Breed Lover's Guide™

RAT TERRIER

A Practical Guide for the Rat Terrier Lover

Judith Tabler

Rat Terrier

Project Team
Editor: Stephanie Fornino
Copy Editor: Joann Woy
Indexer: Dianne L. Schneider
Design: Mary Ann Kahn

T.F.H. Publications, Inc.
One TFH Plaza
Third and Union Avenues
Neptune City, NJ 07753

T.F.H. Publications
President/CEO: Glen S. Axelrod
Executive Vice President: Mark E. Johnson
Publisher: Christopher T. Reggio
Production Manager: Kathy Bontz

Printed and bound in China
11 12 13 14 15 16 1 3 5 7 9 8 6 4 2

Library of Congress Cataloging-in-Publication Data
Tabler, Judith.
  Rat terrier / Judith Tabler.
      p. cm.
  ISBN 978-0-7938-4179-0 (alk. paper)
  1. Rat terrier--Juvenile literature. I. Title.
  SF429.R35T33 2011
  636.755--dc22
                        2010004867

This book has been published with the intent to provide accurate and authoritative information in regard to the subject matter within. While every reasonable precaution has been taken in preparation of this book, the author and publisher expressly disclaim responsibility for any errors, omissions, or adverse effects arising from the use or application of the information contained herein. The techniques and suggestions are used at the reader's discretion and are not to be considered a substitute for veterinary care. If you suspect a medical problem consult your veterinarian.

Note: In the interest of concise writing, "he" is used when referring to puppies and dogs unless the text is specifically referring to females or males. "She" is used when referring to people. However, the information contained herein is equally applicable to both sexes.

The Leader In Responsible Animal Care For Over 50 Years!®
www.tfh.com

Table of Contents

Chapter
1

History of the
Rat Terrier

T he Rat Terrier's history can be traced back several hundred years, but it only achieved status as a recognized breed with the advent of the 21st century. The English word "terrier" appears for the first time in print in Dr. Caius' *Encyclopedia of Dogs*, published in Great Britain in 1570. Dr. Caius noted that these terrier-type dogs were valued by farmers for their ability to catch and kill vermin. Later, terriers were selectively bred to produce long-legged varieties, such as the Airedale Terrier, who hunt rodents and other vermin above ground and through shallow water; short-legged varieties, such as the Skye Terrier and Scottish Terrier, which were to dig down into the ground after their quarry; and the medium-legged variety, which could be used to hunt and to dig. This last variety contains a subgroup that came to be named Feist Terriers.

The Feist Terrier

For many years, the Feist Terrier was considered an American breed, developed in the southeast section of the United States. Some of the earliest references to the Feist Terrier occur in letters and journals written in Virginia and the Carolinas. However, no one was sure where these Feists actually came from— whether they were native American dogs or introduced from Europe.

One long-held theory is that the southeastern Feists are descendants of those dogs who,12,000 years ago, accompanied the ancestors of Native Americans when they crossed the Bering Strait from Asia to North America. A second and opposing theory is that the American Feist dog was descended from dogs brought to the Americas by European explorers and settlers in the 17th and 18th centuries. During the 1990s, scientists at UCLA conducted genetic research on various breeds of dogs,

The Rat Terrier's history can be traced back several hundred years.

Do your homework about dog registration. In recent years, dog registries have become numerous, and some mean absolutely nothing. The primary purpose of a registry is to maintain breeding records of dogs so that breeders can select those dogs who can most improve their respective breeds. You should receive paperwork from your dog's breeder or prior owner that enables your dog to be registered with the United Kennel Club (UKC) or with the American Kennel Club (AKC) as a rare breed. To register your Rat Terrier with his breed club, the Rat Terrier Club of America (RTCA), go to www.ratterrierclub.com or contact the club secretary at rtcaclub@aol.com.

and the DNA results show that current American dog breeds have closer genetic links to European canine bloodlines than to dogs who evolved in Asia. Therefore, the Feist, like many other terriers, probably traces his genetic roots to Great Britain.

The Feist in Great Britain

The English word "terrier" is derived from the Latin word *terra*, meaning ground, and terriers have been important farmyard dogs since the 16th century. Long before poison was available for rodent control, farmers valued terriers for their ability to rid the land of crop-eating mice, rats, rabbits, squirrels, foxes, otters, and even badgers. Farmers in the 16th and 17th centuries selectively bred their terriers for the work they needed the dogs to perform. Few such farmers kept records detailing the ingredients that went into each terrier litter mix. If a puppy grew up to be a prodigious ratter, he was likely added to the next generation of rat-catching genetic "stew."

Most historians who study dogs agree that the Feist-type terrier in Great Britain resulted from a cross between the Smooth Fox Terrier and the black-and-tan Manchester Terrier. In addition, they usually suggest that the Feist's temperament and coat coloring show influence of the now-extinct English White Terrier and the Black and Tan Terrier, among others.

Rat-Fighting Dogs

Feists and other rat-killing dogs were all the rage during the 19th century. For hundreds of years, the British public enjoyed "blood sports," in which dogs were pitted against bears and bulls. However, in 1835, the British Parliament passed the Cruelty to Animals Act, which outlawed bear- and bull-baiting; the law did not, however, condemn rat fighting, so the public turned its attention to that "sport." Rat-fighting dogs became as popular as some of today's human sports figures. Much of the attraction of the rat pits centered on the heavy betting that took place. Records were kept, and favorite dogs were promoted by enterprising fight organizers. The rat fights were well attended by members of all levels of society.

In rat fighting, dogs would be placed in a pit and rats would be dumped in. Spectators would bet on which dog could kill the most rats. One record holder was a white terrier named Billy, who killed 100 rats in five and a half minutes.

The Feist in America

These British rat-catching dogs were prized by American colonists, who brought the little Feist dogs across the Atlantic Ocean. Feists trotted into some of the most illustrious households in

The Rat Terrier is a descendant of the Feist.

WHAT IS A BREED CLUB?

The Rat Terrier breed club is the Rat Terrier Club of America (RTCA). A breed club is an organization formed by people who are interested in preserving a particular breed of dog by selectively breeding dogs to retain a body type and temperament reflective of the original function of the breed. Club members write the breed standard, which defines the ideal dog and against which all dogs are judged. Members of breed clubs who are breeders must subscribe to a strict code of ethics governing breeding practices that will promote healthy puppies. Breed clubs will often provide a contact list of breeders and rescue organizations to prospective dog owners.

the country. In March 1770, George Washington mentions "a small foist looking yellow cur" dog in his diary. Abraham Lincoln writes in 1846 of the "short-legged fice" who follows the larger dogs on a bear hunt. After the bear is killed by the larger dogs, the "fice" arrives on the scene and begins to strut and growl. The little fellow claims the bear for himself, and Lincoln calls the little terrier a "Conceited whelp!"

Breed Crossings

More Feist Terriers were imported throughout the last half of the 19th century, and Americans in the southeastern United States became particularly fond of the handy little dogs. Farmers found them to be first-class ratters, and they crossbred these dogs back to one of the favorite local southern dog breeds: the Smooth Fox Terrier. Hunters took notice of the Feist as well. They crossed him with the Beagle to improve the dog's scenting ability and then with the Whippet and Italian Greyhound for increased speed. Over time, other breeds, including the Chihuahua, Toy Fox Terrier, and Toy Manchester Terrier, joined the mix. These last three crosses reduced the dog's size but increased the coat color palette.

At the beginning of the 20th century, this Americanized Feist terrier once again received attention from an American president. In 1905, President Teddy Roosevelt went on a bear hunt in Colorado, and his guide brought along a small Feist named Skip. Roosevelt wrote letters home to his children describing the little dog. Finally, he brought Skip home, and the little terrier became Archie Roosevelt's constant companion. Skip more than earned his keep once he arrived in Washington, DC.

The Rat Terrier gained much popularity throughout the first half of the 20th century.

The White House was infested with mice and rats: Skip led several other presidential terriers on a race down to the basement, and they cleared those "varmints" out of the place. Teddy Roosevelt heaped praise upon the terrier, and he is credited with giving this newly evolved, Americanized version of the Feist Terrier its new name: the Rat Terrier.

The Rat Terrier Gets His Name
The Rat Terrier gained much popularity throughout the first half of the 20th century, but then, just as suddenly, he fell from favor. Much of this decline was due to the development of effective poisons to control rodents. The Rat Terrier became unemployed and obsolete. In the 1950s, the population of Rat Terriers fell so dramatically that fanciers of the breed worried that their beloved dog might become extinct. There were so few dogs to breed that they crossed their Rat Terriers with the Toy Fox Terrier, Manchester Terrier, Jack/Parson Russell Terriers, and Chihuahuas.

TIMELINE

- **1496:** The terrier is mentioned as a dog type in a book on hunting, *The Boke of St Albans*, by Dame Julianan Berners.

- **1570:** Terrier appears in *Of Englishe Dogges*, by Dr John Caius, published in 1570

- **1770:** George Washington writes of a small foist dog.

- **1820:** Feist Terriers become popular in England.

- **1835:** British Parliament passes Cruelty to Animals Act 1835, outlawing bear- and bull-baiting, which increased the public interest in rat-baiting with terriers.

- **1846:** Abraham Lincoln's poem "Bear Hunt" describes a Feist Terrier.

- **1850–1900:** Increased popularity of Feist Terriers in America.

- **1905:** President Theodore Roosevelt brings Skip to the White House and coins the name Rat Terrier.

- **1920s** and **1930s:** Increased popularity of the Rat Terrier.

- **1950s:** Decline in number of Rat Terriers in the United States; to maintain the breed, fanciers cross breed with Toy Fox Terriers, Manchester Terriers, and Chihuahuas.

- **1958:** The Universal Kennel Club International (UKCI) recognizes the Rat Terrier.

- **1970:** Milton Decker develops a large variety, the "Decker."

- **1972:** American Hairless Terrier whelped.

- **1998:** National Rat Terrier Association (NRTA) creates Chapter Club for Decker.

- **1999:** The Rat Terrier and Teddy Roosevelt Terrier recognized as two separate breeds by the United Kennel Club (UKC).

- **2004:** American Hairless Terrier recognized by the UKC.

- **2004:** AKC admits Rat Terriers into their Foundation Stock Service (FSS).

- **2006:** AKC approves Rat Terriers to participate in Companion Dog Events.

- **2006:** AKC approves Rat Terriers to participate in earthdog events.

- **2010:** Rat Terrier is eligible for the Miscellaneous Class.

By the late 1990s, the resilient Rat Terrier was back. Selective breeding during this period produced two varieties, differentiated by the length of their legs and body. On January 1, 1999, the United Kennel Club (UKC) recognized the shorter-legged, longer-backed dogs as Teddy Roosevelt Terriers and the longer-legged ones as Rat Terriers. Each variety developed a separate breed standard describing the characteristics of a "perfect dog." To encourage the differentiation between the types, breeders no longer crossed Teddy Roosevelt Terriers (Teddies or TRTs) with Rat Terriers. The American Kennel Club (AKC) approved only the Rat Terrier as eligible for the Miscellaneous Class effective June 30, 2010. Regular status will follow 18 months later.

The Decker Terrier and American Hairless Terrier

Two other types of terriers that are closely related to the Rat Terrier should be noted. In 1970, Milton Decker began breeding for a larger Rat Terrier. The Decker Terrier began in 1970, with the crossbreeding of Standard Rat Terriers with various dog breeds, including the Basenji and the Smooth Coated

The AKC approved the Rat Terrier as eligible for the Miscellaneous Class effective June 30, 2010.

Fox Terrier. Continued breeding of larger offspring has resulted in a taller, more muscled dog with a broader, squared-off muzzle. The Decker Terrier is now recognized as a separate strain.

In 1972, the first hairless Rat Terrier was whelped and became the genesis of the American Hairless Terrier, which is now considered a separate breed. Willie and Edwin Scott were delighted to welcome a young, hairless Rat Terrier bitch into their Louisiana home. They named her Josephine. The Scotts were sure that Josephine's hairless trait was a one-time occurrence, a fluke of nature. However, they decided to breed her, and Josephine gave birth to several hairless offspring who became the foundation stock for the breed. A "hairless" puppy is born with short, fuzzy hair that looks different from a regular Rat Terrier's puppy coat. They then begin to lose their hair, and by six to eight weeks, they are truly hairless. Their skin is pink and spotted. The number of American Hairless Terriers has increased due to the selective breeding of dogs who carry the recessive hairless gene.

Both the Decker Terrier and the American Hairless Terrier are recognized as separate breeds by several canine clubs such as the UKC and by the Universal Kennel Club International (UKCI), but they are not yet accepted by the AKC.

In 1972, the first hairless Rat Terrier was whelped.

Characteristics of
Your Rat Terrier

Although the Rat Terrier has a long history in the United States, it was only recently that the fanciers of the breed decided to analyze and describe the ideal conformation of the Rat Terrier. In so doing, the Rat Terrier Club of America (RTCA) established an official breed standard. This standard is important because it gives the breeder a blueprint for the breed. This sounds easier than it is. Many Rat Terrier fanciers had to discuss and agree upon how they wished the ideal Rat Terrier to look. The first and overriding concern examined was the historical function of the breed and how the dog evolved to best suit this role. The dog's physical characteristics, from his teeth to the tip of his tail, were analyzed and debated until a descriptive picture of the "perfect" Rat Terrier emerged.

When they established this breed standard, the RTCA narrowed the definition of the breed. They excluded Teddy Roosevelt Terriers and the American Hairless Terriers from the breed. Puppies resulting from crossbreeding to those two varieties were no longer considered purebred Rat Terriers. As a result, the Teddy Roosevelt Terrier and the American Hairless Terrier have now developed separate breed standards of their own.

Physical Characteristics

If you have ever been to a dog show or seen one on television, you may have wondered exactly what that judge is looking for when she examines a dog. The judge is trained to know the breed's standard, and she then compares the show dog to that standard.

If you were judging a Rat Terrier, you would first watch him come into the ring and then ask him to be placed on the judging table. You, as the judge, would

Although the Rat Terrier has a long history in the United States, it was only recently that the fanciers of the breed decided to analyze and describe the ideal conformation of the Rat Terrier.

In 1985, Benjamin L. Hart, DVM, and Lynette A. Hart, PhD, published an article entitled "Selecting Pet Dogs on the Basis of Cluster Analysis of Breed Behavior Profiles and Gender" in the *Journal of the American Veterinary Medical Association,* 186:1181–1185 (1985). The authors surveyed veterinarians and dog obedience judges with questions relating to behavior characteristics of 56 American Kennel Club (AKC)-recognized breeds. A summary of their research states that terriers were bred to seek and instantly kill vermin without specific human direction. Terriers are a type of dog that has not been bred to follow human commands as they carry out their tasks. In contrast, herding dogs, such as Shetland Sheepdogs, were trained to respond to human commands as they work in the fields. The study concluded that the historic work requirements, conditioning factors, selective breeding, and training for terriers has resulted in dogs who have low to medium trainability, are highly reactive, and are somewhat more aggressive than other dog types.

want to determine if the size of the dog is correct according to the standard.

It is important to remember that the characteristics of body structure described in this section are for the perfect Rat Terrier. An individual dog will vary from this standard in several points. That is what makes judging so difficult. You might find one dog with a wonderful head and nice topline, but his legs are a little too short, and you don't like the shape of his feet. The next dog has the perfect length of legs and a good topline, but the proportion of the head is slightly off. The third dog is great, but his back is a little short, and he doesn't gait as easily as the others. The fourth dog's bite is level and his only white spot is just about the

size of a quarter. This goes on and on as you go from one dog to the next. It is up to you, the judge, to decide which dog is closest to the perfect dog described in the standard. Some judges will give the blue ribbon to the first one, with the nice head and topline but short legs, but another judge could decide differently. That is what makes showing a dog an adventure. No one can be sure which dogs will be in the ring that day, and no one ever knows how the judge will decide every time she meets a different group of dogs.

Size
As a conformation show judge, first you would inspect the dogs for size. For Rat Terriers, the breed standard specifies two

sizes: the Miniature and the Standard. A miniature Rat Terrier includes dogs who, when measured at the shoulder, stand between 10 and 13 inches (25.5 cm). The standard Rat Terrier has a shoulder height measurement between 13 and 19 inches (33 and 48.5 cm). The average weights for either variety are not mentioned in the standard, but a Rat Terrier will weigh between 10 and 25 pounds (4.5 kg and 11.5 kg). The miniature and standard-sized dogs are not separated in dog show classes until they are 12 months old. If someone offers you a toy or a giant Rat Terrier, you should realize that neither variety is recognized by the Rat Terrier Club of America (RTCA).

Coat

Next, you would inspect the dog's coat. The Rat Terrier's proper coat is short and dense. The coat should never be rough or wiry, like that of some other terrier breeds. And the coat must look healthy: smooth and shiny.

Coat Color

Now, look at the color of the coat. Although Rat Terriers can come in many colors, some colors are preferred and others will disqualify the dog from competition. Most dogs fall into the tri-colored range, white with black and tan or rust; or bicolored, which is white with black or white with tan. Preferably, white

Some Rat Terriers are bicolored, which is white with black or white with tan.

will cover 20 to 90 percent of the dog's body. However, dogs can come in varying shades of chocolate, red, orange, lemon, or blue. It is acceptable to have tan points or trim on the cheeks, eyebrows, eye dots, chest, vent, legs, and the inside of the ears. The location of these markings is similar to the way a Doberman Pinscher is marked. The colors should be well defined, not faded or muddied. The judge will look closely at a dark-colored dog because she must find at least a quarter-sized amount of white somewhere on his body—not just on his paws or face. Dogs with albinism, with brindle or merle coats, or any bicolor without that prerequisite amount of white are considered mismarked.

Head

At this point, you would judge the dog's head. The shape of the head should be fairly long and wedge shaped. The nose should be broad enough to not be too pointy or "snipy." The standard states that the head should have certain proportions. Check that the length from the nose to the "stop" (where the head rises up from the muzzle) is slightly shorter or of equal length to the distance from the stop back to the occiput (the back section of the top dog's head just before the neck—it can be a prominent bump in some breeds).

Nose

In Rat Terriers, the nose is normally black, but a lighter nose color is permitted when it matches the eye rim.

Eyes

The eyes of the Rat Terrier should be rounded or slightly almond shaped. They should be brown or hazel. On chocolate or blue-colored dogs, the eyes can be lighter and even amber, but blue eyes or walleyes (one blue and one brown) are disqualifications.

Ears

No judge can look at the Rat Terrier's head without noting those splendid ears. They must be V-shaped, but they can be upright (pricked), tipped (semi-pricked

The Rat Terrier has distinctive V-shaped ears.

ears that fold halfway and fall forward), or button (rise only slightly and then fold forward). Check to make sure that the ears are a matched set. One cannot be pricked and the other semi-pricked.

Jaw

The dog's jaw must be hinged so that it could easily carry small game, and the lips should be clean and tight. The teeth should be evenly spaced, and a scissors bite (like most people's) is preferred, but an even bite is acceptable. Teeth that are

The Rat Terrier's hips and thighs must be muscular and powerful.

badly out of line and undershot (like a Bulldog) or overshot (the reverse jaw of a Bulldog) are disqualifications.

Neck

Moving back from the head, run your hands down the dog's neck. It should arch slightly at the crest and be firm and muscular, with no loose skin except for the wrinkle under the jaw.

Chest

Feel the chest; it must be oval shaped and broad, but you should be able to see and feel the breastbone. The lower part of the chest (the brisket) should be large enough so that it extends near or below the dog's elbows, allowing plenty of room for the lungs. The shoulders should be set back and long, but proper ones will fit fairly close together near the top so that the front legs can swing easily when the Rat Terrier trots.

Rib Cage

Slide your hands over the rib cage. The Rat Terrier's ribs should feel long and well sprung to permit expansion but then taper as they progress back toward the rear.

Hindquarters

Next, run your hand down the hindquarters. The hips and thighs must be muscular and powerful.

Puppy Love

HOW TO SELECT A PUPPY

I always recommend meeting the mother dog when you go to select a puppy. Up to about the age of seven weeks, the mother is usually the biggest influence in a pup's life. She passes along her disposition, as well as her genes. Since the 1950s, prospective dog owners have tried to figure out what puppy traits correlate with desirable adult dog traits, but they are only guides and not foolproof. The following tests are sometimes used on puppies who are seven weeks old. However, remember that you will often be able to improve a puppy's responses on a temperament test by good handling and life experiences.

1. **Social Attraction:** Social attraction to people, confidence, or dependence.

2. **Following:** Willingness to follow a person.

3. **Restraint:** Degree of dominant or submissive tendency and ease of handling in difficult situations.

4. **Social Dominance:** Degree of acceptance of social dominance by a person.

5. **Elevation:** Degree of accepting dominance while in a position of no control, such as at the veterinarian or groomer's.

6. **Retrieving:** Degree of willingness to do something for you. Together with Social Attraction and Following, a key indicator for ease or difficulty in training.

7. **Touch Sensitivity:** Degree of sensitivity to touch and a key indicator to the type of training equipment required.

8. **Sound Sensitivity:** Degree of sensitivity to sound, such as loud noises or thunderstorms.

9. **Sight Sensitivity:** Degree of response to a moving object, such as chasing bicycles, children, or squirrels.

10. **Stability:** Degree of startle response to a strange object.

Topline

Take a step back and look at the topline of the dog. A well-shaped Rat Terrier will be moderately long and almost level. The tail needs to flow naturally along the topline, but it can be carried horizontal or almost erect. The tail should be docked, shorter than a Fox Terrier's, and tapered.

Legs and Feet

Move your gaze to the legs and feet. The front legs should be nearly straight up and down. The back legs should have moderately bent stifles that turn out slightly. The hocks should be low and firm. It is preferred that there are no dewclaws, but they may occur on the front legs. Look at the paws. Rat Terriers should have compact, oval feet with arched toes, with strong nails and tough pads. The front feet point straight forward, but the back ones can point out slightly. This allows the dog to anchor himself when cornering prey.

Gait

Now that you have gone all over the dog, you need to see him move. His

The Rat Terrier should be active and alert.

CHARACTERISTICS CHECKLIST

The following are the AKC's list of acceptable colors and markings for Rat Terriers:

Colors:
- ✔ black & white
- ✔ black, tan, & white
- ✔ black, white, & tan
- ✔ blue, white, & tan
- ✔ red, white, & tan
- ✔ white
- ✔ white & apricot
- ✔ white & black
- ✔ white & blue

- ✔ white & blue fawn
- ✔ white & chocolate
- ✔ white & fawn
- ✔ white & lemon
- ✔ white & red
- ✔ white & silver
- ✔ white & tan
- ✔ white, black, & tan
- ✔ white, chocolate, & tan

Markings:
- ✔ badger markings
- ✔ blanket—on back
- ✔ Irish marked
- ✔ piebald
- ✔ sable, white markings
- ✔ solid
- ✔ spotted or patched
- ✔ white markings, tan points
- ✔ white mask, white markings

gait should be lively and easy. You do not want to see a dog who trots with a hackneyed gait like a Miniature Pinscher or with a rolling gait like a Bulldog. The Rat Terrier movement should be jaunty and agile. It should say to a judge, "Look at me. I am a great Rat Terrier."

Living With a Rat Terrier

The breed standard for the Rat Terrier lists what qualities are desirable for the ideal temperament. Part of the description says that the Rat Terrier should be active and alert, responsive, friendly, faithful, protective, and somewhat standoffish. They should never be excessively shy or aggressive. Yikes, that is a lot of adjectives for such a little dog! But for the most part, Rat Terriers live up to them.

Temperament

In general, Rat Terriers are considered to be less aggressive and more levelheaded than some of their terrier cousins. This personality is probably due to the "calmer" breeds added to the Rat Terrier's genetic pool. The Rat Terrier's temperament also is shaped in part by the amount of socialization he receives as a puppy. If you expect your puppy to be calm around strangers, make sure that he meets a lot of strangers who become friends. If you want a dog to tolerate cats, introduce him to cats early. On the

MULTIPLE DOGS

A Rat Terrier owner who has had several dogs over a period of years told me recently that she deliberately got one Rat Terrier before the other (from two different litters), rather than two at the same time. She made this choice because she wanted them to bond to her more than to each other. When she got two at the same time, she felt that the two pups formed a kind of pack together, and it took a while for them to include her. I am not sure that this is everyone's experience, but it is worth considering when you are thinking of getting two dogs.

other hand, it is almost impossible to overcome some dogs' hunting instinct. Things that flee and squeak are generally seen as prey and are quickly dispatched. You must make sure that your young Rat Terrier understands that your kittens and other pets are part of his family.

Overall, the Rat Terrier's devoted fans are quick to note that his temperament is all terrier—lively, playful, determined, and loyal to a fault. He is happy curled up in your lap, but he is always alert, and a quick movement can send him charging across the room in pursuit of any kind of varmint—real or imaginary.

Companionability With Children

Most Rat Terriers are good with children, but early socialization is important in this area as well. Small children can be threatening to a small dog. No dog likes to be put in an environment where he is poked and pulled. It is up to you to make sure that your Rat Terrier has good

experiences with children early so that he accepts them and learns to live with them. Once he decides that a child is part of his family unit, he will be just as loyal and dedicated to the child as to any other family member. In fact, he may become even more dedicated once both dog and child figure out some games to play. Rat Terriers are always up for a fun game.

Companionability With Dogs and Other Pets

Part of your "head of the pack" duties will include socializing your Rat Terrier to any other pets in the household. It is important to remember that the characteristics of temperament and body structure described here are for the *average* Rat Terrier. An individual dog will vary. Some of this will be due to breeding, and some will be due to the way the pup was raised. The old debate of nurture versus nature applies not only to human beings; it applies to our four-legged friends as well. Generally, Rat Terriers do well with other animals in the household.

Pack Leadership

Rat Terriers have strong personalities, and their owners need to be accepted as the "pack leader." Put simply, the Rat Terrier needs to know that you are the boss, top dog, head honcho, alpha dog. This position of dominance must be earned by gaining the dog's respect through consistent and gentle authority—not through physical strength. Once this is established, your Rat Terrier will do almost anything to please you. He will become a dedicated and worshipping follower.

Trainability

Rat Terriers are quick to learn and relatively easy to train. They are born problem solvers and they love games. If you can tap into these traits when you are training, you will have a happy and eager student. The key is to start with simple commands and reward your dog whenever he is successful in completing the task. Do not move on to more complicated tasks until your dog has mastered the easier ones. The idea is to set up training exercises so that you can reward his achievements, not punish his mistakes. Rat Terriers will do almost anything for food treats and for praise from their favorite humans.

Environment

Rat Terriers are adaptable dogs, and they can live almost anywhere—city, country, or suburbia. All they need is someone to provide them with affection and exercise. They love to go on walks and to romp in the yard or park with their favorite people. They are not dogs who should be left out in the yard for extended periods because they crave human companionship. Being with their human is what makes their clocks tick, and if they are left out in a yard for long periods of time they will find other ways to amuse themselves. Barking and digging are two alleviators of doggy boredom that come to mind.

Exercise Requirements

Rat Terriers are not large dogs, but they require regular exercise. In addition to short walks to make sure that your dog does his "business" outside, you should plan on a 20- to 30-minute walk in the morning and again in the afternoon to keep your dog happy and in shape. Rat Terriers thrive with activity and stimulation. A brisk walk on a leash is a wonderful way to channel some of your dog's energy.

Chapter 3

Supplies for Your Rat Terrier

O nce you have decided that a Rat Terrier is the dog breed for you, you have to ready your home for the new addition. You will need some supplies, and while you may not want to purchase every item initially, it is a good idea to have some of the basics ready when your dog arrives. Experienced Rat Terrier owners suggest some of the following items.

Attire

Consider the weather in your area. Because your Rat Terrier has a short single coat, he may not tolerate cold well. If your dog shivers and snuggles down under layers of fabric (towels, blankets, or whatever he can wiggle under), consider getting him a dog sweater. Many owners enjoy dressing their Rat Terriers in clothing, but others balk at garbing their four-footed friends in something that is "too cute." However, if you live in a cold climate, dog jackets and sweaters are not just for comfort and looks but also for your dog's health—and potty training if you are taking him outside. A constantly chilled dog is neither a healthy dog nor a well-exercised dog.

Baby Gates

You may want to limit your dog to certain rooms or keep him from going up or down stairs. Baby gates work well for most dogs, but a small puppy can often scoot

Because of his short single coat, your Rat Terrier may not tolerate cold well, and he may need to wear a jacket or sweater.

underneath them. A better choice is a gate made especially for dogs, and there are many styles from which to choose. These gates can be free-standing, screwed into the wall, or pressure mounted, which means that the tension from a spring holds the gate in place. Make sure that the bars on the gate are close enough together so that the pup cannot get his head stuck. If you have a young pup or a dog who likes to chew, a wooden gate may not be the best choice. And don't think that a small dog like a Rat Terrier needs a low gate;

your dog will be able to jump, so pick out one that is at least 30 inches (76 cm)— even higher for an enthusiastic adult dog who likes to spring up.

Bed

Next, you will need a bed for your dog. If you have a puppy or a dog who is not yet housetrained, a nice soft towel can make a great first bed. Like many short-haired breeds, Rat Terriers love to curl up in a bed, using it like a nest. If you are using a crate, you might want to begin by putting some old towels inside it. Some dogs seem to enjoy shaping their "nests," and towels are soft and easily pushed around into a comfy bed. In addition, they are absorbent and washable. Keep the towels clean and check them often for chewed spots and tears. Towels are for beds, not snacks.

Dogs, just like people, have preferences for various positions when they sleep. Watch your dog sleep. Once you have some idea of how he likes to sleep, you can invest in a more expensive bed that suits his sleeping style. Some dogs continue to scratch up towels and blankets to form a nest, so they might be happiest with nice pieces of strong fleece or blankets. Others like a soft flat bed to stretch out on, so you can find a doggy-sized mattress made of foam or one filled with a variety of materials. I have one dog who likes a flat bed because she hangs her head off the edge. Another one sleeps with his head propped up, so he prefers a bed with an edge around it. This edged bed also works for the dog who likes to curl up in a little ball.

Collar

Your pup should get used to wearing a collar while he is still young. A lightweight nylon collar works well for a Rat Terrier— it is light enough for a small dog but strong enough for a terrier. Size the collar carefully. It must fit snugly so that it will

Ask the Expert

While either collars and harnesses are excellent choices for most Rat Terriers, Carmeta French of Warren Mountain Rat Terriers cautions that only a harness should be used on a Rat Terrier who might be at risk for an inherited health issue called primary lens luxation, which affects the eye. (See Chapter 9: Health of Your Rat Terrier.) Many canine ophthalmologists worry that this eye condition can be aggravated when the dog strains against a collar.

not slip off, but it should not be tight. You should be able to easily slide your finger inside the collar. Do this often if your pup or dog is growing or is gaining or losing weight. Another word of warning about collars: Each year, dogs are strangled by collars that get caught on fences, branches, furniture, ventilation grates, and anything else that can snag a collar or a tag dangling from a collar. Sometimes one dog will pull another dog around by biting the collar. This may begin as play but can end in tragedy.

One way to prevent this is to purchase a collar with a breakaway feature. This kind of collar is sometimes harder to find, but look for one of two types. The first has an elastic section that stretches when a lot of pressure is applied and allows the dog to slip free. The second kind has a plastic connector that will release if sufficient pressure is applied. Select the one that works best for your dog's environment and personality.

Some Rat Terriers have very sensitive necks and do better with a soft type of collar that is called either a hound or martingale collar. These can be hard to find in pet stores, but they are available on online pet shopping sites.

Crate

A crate is one of the first items you need for your Rat Terrier. Many novice dog owners balk at the idea of a crate, but from the dog's point of view, the confined space is like a cozy den. Dogs and puppies like to have a place where they can curl up in security and privacy.

Types of Crates

Crates come in four basic types: wood, wire, metal, and plastic. The wood ones are expensive, heavy, and can be difficult to clean. The wire ones are easy to clean and provide good ventilation for the dog, but their openness can eliminate the cozy, den-like feeling. People often drape a blanket or towel over the wire crate to make it more cave-like. However, I have had dogs who spend their time chewing these coverings and gnawing off pieces of fabric. Metal crates are easy to clean and can be a good choice, but they can

One of the first items you will need is a crate.

CHEWING

All puppies need to chew while they are teething. Chewing stimulates the gums and eases the pain of teething. Therefore, don't scold your puppy for chewing. Instead, protect your house from puppy damage and give him acceptable items to chew, like a Nylabone. My dogs like dampened and then frozen washcloths. They are inexpensive and easily replaced. Keep an eye on them though—you don't want your dog ripping off chunks or long threads that can get lodged in his throat.

retain heat in warm weather and stay cool in cold weather. Plastic or Plexiglas crates seems to work best for me. They are lightweight, easy to clean, and work well in most temperatures.

Crate Size

How big should your dog's crate be? A crate must be big enough so that your dog can easily stand up in it and turn around. If you have a puppy, you may need to invest in two crates because you don't want the puppy's first crate to be too large. Crates are terrific aids as you begin to housetrain your new Rat Terrier because most dogs do not want to soil where they sleep. If the crate is too large, your pup may claim one section as his sleeping area and might use the excess space to eliminate in. You want this first crate to be big enough to be a bedroom, not a master suite with private bathroom.

Crate Use

The crate often becomes a sleeping area and safety zone for a dog. He should understand that it is a good place to crawl into for a nap or quiet time. He can also be put in his crate when something is going on in the house that you want him to be kept away from. For example, I find it useful to put my dogs in crates if a workman is around for some reason. I have found that workmen are apt to leave doors open as they go in and out, and my dogs are geniuses at whipping out a door left open for even a few seconds. However, you must remember that the crate is not a place to leave a dog for long periods. I strongly advise that you never confine your dog for more than three hours at a time—and even less time for puppies.

A final word on crates. Crate your dog while he is riding in your car. We all know that people need to be belted in while traveling in a car to keep from flying forward if the car stops quickly. An anchored dog crate will do the same thing for your dog.

Ex-Pen

If you don't have a room that works well to confine your dog, consider an exercise pen or ex-pen. Ex-pens are like a child's playpen, but for a dog. They are useful for those times when you need your dog to be kept someplace safe but not necessarily confined to his crate.

Food and Water Bowls

You will need two sturdy bowls for your dog's food and water. Puppies tend to think of bowls as something to bat around, and although you will discourage this, unbreakable bowls are usually best. While ceramic ones may be decorative, look for sturdy plastic or stainless steel bowls. Plastic is chewable, can harbor bacteria, and is a little harder to clean than stainless steel, so I usually select the metal ones. Wash the bowls regularly. Even if your Rat Terrier gobbles up every drop, wash the bowl after each feeding. I wash the water bowl at the same time because that is an easy way to be sure that the water is changed regularly too.

Grooming Supplies

You will want to have some grooming tools on hand for your new Rat Terrier. The basics include a bristle brush, a curry brush, and a grooming glove to remove superficial dirt and loose dead hair. You'll also need a flea comb, which has narrow teeth and will help you check for flea and flea dirt. Dog shampoo, a spray hose, towels, and a nonslip mat for washing and drying your dog are also necessary, as are cotton balls to wipe our your Rat Terrier's ears and nail trimmers to keep those sharp nails short. Oral care products, such as canine toothpaste and a toothbrush, should be purchased too. A more complete list and explanation of the use of these tools is covered in Chapter 5: Grooming Your Rat Terrier.

You will need two sturdy bowls for your dog's food and water.

SUPPLY EXPENSES

It's easy to spend a lot of money on dog supplies if you want to. But other than the items relating to your dog's safety (the crate, collar, leash, and identification tags) and basic functions (eating, drinking, and sleeping), proceed slowly. There is no need to run out and purchase every cute toy you see. Try one or two and see how they work for your Rat Terrier. Once you find some he likes, don't put them all out at once because most dogs only seem to respond to a few toys at a time.

Harness and Halter

Some people prefer to use a harness on their Rat Terrier. A harness crosses underneath the dog's body. Many different types and styles of harnesses are available; some harnesses clasp in just one spot, while others attach in two or more places. There are also "step-in" harnesses that are designed so that the dog can just walk into them. Make sure that the harness you choose does not interfere with your dog's movement or come up on the neck, where it can injure his trachea. Also examine the straps. You don't want any rough or sharp edges that will rub against your dog, nor do you want a harness that is so heavy your four-footed companion won't enjoy your walks together.

Halters resemble harnesses but have a strap that encircles the dog's nose. However, a halter is not to be confused with a muzzle: A dog with a halter can drink, bark, yawn, and eat his treats. A halter works well for those dogs who continue to pull on lead, but it is something a dog needs to get acquainted with because most resist having something around their noses.

Identification

Even if you keep your dog's tags firmly attached to his collar, he can still get lost. The best defense for this is to microchip your dog so that he is easily identified when found. A microchip is a computer chip that is about the size of a grain of rice. A veterinarian implants the chip between the dog's shoulder blades using a special syringe. The process is almost painless and provides your dog with a lifetime of protection. The code in the microchip can be scanned at animal shelters and veterinarian hospitals, and it will tell his rescuers the name of the dog's registered owner.

Leash

The best leash for your Rat Terrier is either a 4- or 6-foot one (1.2- to 1.8-m), depending upon how much of it you want to curl up in your hand when you have your dog walking close to you. The leash should be light and strong. Leather is good and long lasting if cared for properly, but a nylon or cotton webbed lead is easier to care for and dries more quickly than leather if you get caught outside in the rain. The leash should be comfortable for you to hold and not so heavy that the weight is unpleasant for your dog. Do not let your dog chew on his leash; it is not his toy. If chewing becomes a problem, temporarily switch to a light chain lead. Chain leads are not comfortable for your hands, but they don't taste good either. A retractable leash can be fun when you want to give your dog some extra freedom, but they do not work well for training or with an aggressive dog.

No matter what type of leash you choose, make sure that the snap that attaches it to your dog's collar is strong, secure, and easy to use.

Your dog's tags must be attached to his collar.

SUPPLIES CHECKLIST

- ✓ collar
- ✓ crate or two (one for the home and one for the car)
- ✓ dog bed
- ✓ exercise pen or ex-pen
- ✓ food and water bowls
- ✓ gate or gates
- ✓ grooming supplies
- ✓ ID tags/microchip
- ✓ leash
- ✓ toys

Toys

Rat Terriers love toys, but not all toys love Rat Terriers. When selecting a toy for your dog, try to think like a Rat Terrier. That wonderful, adorable (and sometimes expensive) toy you just brought home means one thing to most Rat Terriers: prey. Ribbons, bells, plastic eyes, noses, and whatever other doodads are attached to that cute little toy are simply something to be ripped off, chewed up, and sometimes swallowed. The innards (stuffing) are meant to be ripped out and sometimes eaten, as well. And when it comes to getting eaten, rope toys aren't a whole lot better than plush toys: Only let your Rat Terrier play tug-of-war with a rope toy when you are around to supervise because strands of rope can be ingested and may not pass through the digestive system.

Tennis balls are common toys for dogs,

but not in our house. I write this as the owner of a terrier who has required three surgeries to remove chunks of tennis balls from his intestine. We try to be careful, but our neighbor built a tennis court illegally close to our yard, and as vigilant as I try to be, Tosh has managed to find some of the balls that I've missed.

Similarly, rawhide chews are often advised against because some dogs gulp down chunks that are too big to swallow, and these can become lodged in the dog's throat. Supervise your Rat Terrier if you give him rawhide chews.

Rat Terriers often do best with hard rubber toys. The most popular models are those with hollow insides where you can tuck treats. Rat Terriers are puzzle solvers, and trying to get those snacks out is entertaining for the dog—and his human spectators. As with any dog toy, however, examine rubber toys periodically for signs of wear. The rubber can become brittle with time and break off more easily.

Chapter
4

Feeding Your
Rat Terrier

Your Rat Terrier depends on you to provide him with a healthy, well-balanced diet. When you acquire your puppy or new dog, be sure to find out what his breeder or prior owner has been feeding him and try to maintain the same diet for several days. Think of it as "comfort food" for this new member of the family, who has to adjust to a brand-new lifestyle in your home. Sudden changes in food can cause stomach upsets, something both you and your new dog will want to avoid. Once your Rat Terrier has settled in, you can determine if his food is the best for him. The optimum way to introduce new food is to mix it in with the old, a little at time, gradually increasing the percentage of the new food.

The Building Blocks of Nutrition

Dog food needs to contain nutrients that are properly balanced for all dogs in general and for your Rat Terrier in particular. In addition to water, dogs need food that gives them carbohydrates, fats, minerals, proteins, and vitamins. The amount of each varies according to your dog's age, activity level, and overall health.

Puppies need special attention, so be sure to select a food appropriate for growing dogs. Puppy food needs to be higher in protein and fat than adult food.

Your dog needs a nutritious diet to stay happy and healthy.

The protein content of puppy food should be around 33 percent, and the fat content at about 20 percent.

Ask your dog's veterinarian for recommendations on the best type of food for your Rat Terrier.

Carbohydrates

Carbohydrates are a source of energy. The exact amount needed is determined by your dog's lifestyle and activity level because excessive amounts of

FEEDING A PUPPY

Ahealthy Rat Terrier puppy will be weaned and ready to go to his new home when he is about eight weeks old. He will reach his adult size somewhere between 7 to 12 months, and good feeding practices are important for his proper growth and health. His food intake should be determined by his energy needs. Energy needs are determined by the dog's age, activity level, breed type, and temperament. No one can say exactly how much your puppy should be fed without understanding how active he is on a daily (sometimes hourly) basis. A rough guideline is that an active puppy should be fed about twice what an adult dog who weighs the same amount would eat. Therefore, if your four-month-old puppy weighs 8 pounds (3.5 kg), he could be expected to need twice what an 8-pound (3.5-kg) adult would eat. However, because there are so many variables in your puppy's environment and lifestyle, you need to handle him every day to check his health. He should not be too thin or too fat. Plump puppies may be cute, but studies show that an overweight pup can often develop into an obese adult dog.

carbohydrates contribute to obesity.

Fats
Fats are important in animal diets because they provide energy, carry fat-soluble vitamins, and add flavor and texture. They also assist in maintaining a dog's optimum skin and coat condition.

Minerals
Minerals (and vitamins) are necessary for optimum bone formation, muscle development, correct fluid balance, cell structure, and nervous system function.

Proteins
Proteins are amino acids that are commonly found in animal sources, such as meat and meat by-products. Proteins are necessary to metabolize food into energy and to maintain the optimum hormone levels that control many body functions.

Vitamins
Vitamins (and minerals) are needed so that the dog can absorb fats and carbohydrates and for the many other chemical reactions in the body. It is important that these nutrients are

Ask the Expert

Even the most experienced Rat Terrier owners don't always agree on the whether to feed their dogs on a schedule or let their dogs have access to food all day (known as "free feeding"). Carmeta French of Warren Mountain Rat Terriers in Vermont feeds her puppies three to four times a day in scheduled intervals so that their outside potty breaks will be easy to predict. The first meal is in the morning while her family gets ready for school/work and then the pups go on a walk. A second feeding is around lunchtime, again followed by a walk. The third feeding and follow-on walk is after school, around three in the afternoon. The final feeding and walk takes place just before bedtime. Her adults eat twice a day: once in the morning and the other is after school.

On the other hand, Pam Mills, Rat Terrier fancier and Secretary of the Rat Terrier Club of America (RTCA), lets her adult dogs free-feed. She says that "Rats like to graze on kibble." Her dogs have a habit of grabbing a mouthful of kibble, carrying to wherever she is, spitting it out, and then leisurely eating it near her. As she says, "They don't want to miss any time with their person"—or the possibility of any action.

balanced in the proper amounts and ratios.

Water

A dog's body is approximately 70 percent water. Water is important in turning food into energy, sustaining a normal body temperature, removing toxins, replacing expelled fluids, carrying nutrients throughout the body, and maintaining healthy blood.

Feeding Schedules

Give your puppy four small meals a day until he is about four months old and then gradually reduce the number to three and to two by the time he is about a year old. After that you can determine a schedule for your Rat Terrier. While an adult dog can do fine on one daily meal, many breeders and owners prefer to split the meal into two feedings—for both small and large dogs. Your Rat Terrier will do best with a regular schedule, so pick feeding times that you can adhere to on a daily basis. My terriers eat their food promptly, but I have known some dogs who like to prolong their meals. I usually pick up any leftover food after about 20 minutes to encourage them to pay attention to mealtime.

While I prefer scheduling my dog's feedings, other owners leave food out all the time and let their dog eat whenever he wishes. This is called "free-feeding," and it works well as long as the dog maintains a healthy weight. However, it is not advised for a dog who is apt to overeat or for a multi-dog household where the dogs are not content to share the food equally. Free-feeding also limits your choice of food because it can only be used with foods, such as kibble, that can remain out in the air for several hours.

Commercial Diets

Three basic types of commercial dog food are available: dry, canned, and semi-moist.

When buying dog food, remember that you get what your pay for. Not all dog foods are the same. You can classify them into three categories: popular, premium, and generic. Popular-grade dog food is the most common and is sold in supermarkets. The ingredients are adequate for nutrition and are palatable to dogs. The premium grade is manufactured to provide optimal nutrition at different stages of your dog's life. These products state on their packaging that they are designed for pets of certain ages and activity levels. Premium-grade dog food is apt to be sold through veterinarians, pet stores, or feed stores, and it is generally more costly than popular dog food. Generic or private-label dog food is lower in cost than the other choices and contains less-expensive ingredients. Some tests have shown that these less-expensive brands have less nutrients and are not as digestible for dogs.

Dry Food (Kibble)

Most dog food sold in the United States is dry food or kibble. Kibble is sold in bags

Kibble is sold in bags and can come in various forms.

READING DOG FOOD LABELS

Take your eyeglasses to the store and read those dog food labels when selecting dinner for your Rat Terrier. If you aren't comfortable with a little basic math, take your calculator too. Compare the protein, fat, and fiber on different labels to get an idea of which food is best for your dog. These nutrients are based on dry-matter measurements. The label on a can of dog food might read: Protein 8.0%, Fat 3.0%, Fiber 1.0%, Moisture 82.0%. This can of food contains 82% moisture; thus, it contains 18% dry matter. To determine the dry-matter nutrient content, you must figure the label's nutrient percentage multiplied by 100 percent and then divide that by the dry-matter percentage (18%).

Protein = 8 x 100 ÷ 18 = 44.4%

Fat = 3 x 100 ÷ 18 = 16.6%

Fiber = 1 x 100 ÷ 18 = 5.5%

Additional information on the label often includes:

- a guaranteed analysis (but this statement does not really tell you the quality of the food)

- ingredients, which are listed in the descending order of weight

- feeding guidelines, which you may need to adjust according to your individual dog

- nutritional adequacy statement; most manufacturers rely on the Association of American Feed Control's (AAFCO) recommendations

and can come in various forms, such as meal, chunks, or shaped bits. Numerous brands and a variety of flavors are available. If you select kibble for your Rat Terrier, read the information on the bag to make sure that the label states that the food is nutritionally balanced to meet the needs of your dog at his stage of life. The label should state that this information is a "guaranteed analysis." Find a brand that lists its protein source first—this should be meat, and not meat by-products. Finding a protein such as meat listed first helps you avoid products that have fillers as a primary ingredient.

Dry food is the most popular form of dog food, and it includes kibble and most dog biscuits. Dry food is not totally "dry." Most labels reveal that each bag contains somewhere between 6 and 12 percent moisture. Dry food is actually a dough that has been baked and cut or broken into edible pieces. Ingredients in dry food often include cereal grains; meat, poultry, or fish products; and milk products. During the baking stage, some vitamins can be lost, and the better dog food manufacturers add supplemental vitamins.

Kibble appeals to many dog owners because it is convenient and economical, but do not be swayed into buying huge lower-cost bags if your dog will not finish the contents in a week or two. Dry dog food contains oils that can go rancid when exposed to air or heat. When this happens, the beneficial vitamins and minerals may be destroyed. Always store kibble in a clean, cool, dry location.

To have the best of both worlds, many Rat Terriers do well on a combination of kibble and canned food. This raises the amount of protein they receive while also providing some grain and vegetable matter in the diet; because dogs are omnivores, they need both meat and plant-based food.

Always read the label to be sure that your Rat Terrier is getting the nutrition he needs.

FOOD ALLERGIES

Rat Terriers have been known to develop allergies to some foods. Allergies can develop at any stage of your dog's life, so just because he could tolerate some dietary element last month does not mean that he cannot become hypersensitive to it now. The good news is that most dogs develop hypersensitivity (also called a pruritic reaction) to only one or two ingredients. Your best defense is to pay attention to your dog's condition. A dry, itchy coat is often an indication of an allergic reaction. If your veterinarian concurs that food allergy is the cause, you will have to place your dog on an "elimination diet." This diet will present your dog with foods that are not common allergy triggers, such as fish and potatoes. Your dog will eat this controlled meal for several weeks so that you can see if there is any improvement. If he does improve, you can gradually introduce suspected allergy-provoking foods, one ingredient at a time. When the symptoms reappear, you will have a clear diagnosis and know exactly what ingredient is causing your dog's misery.

Canned Food

Canned food is also popular with lots of Rat Terriers, and many people deem it a better choice than either semi-moist foods or kibble. Canned food is high in protein and fats, and it contains fewer chemical additives, artificial colors, and preservatives than other food types. On the other hand, this type of food is more costly than dry foods, and it contains 70 to 82 percent moisture—basically, expensive water. This moisture, however, makes canned food easily digestible. Because canned food is manufactured by pouring various ingredients into cans, which are then cooked, some nutrients are lost in processing. Reputable manufacturers usually add supplements to replace the lost nutritional content.

The cooking and canning process means that excessive amounts of preservatives are unnecessary, but canned food will spoil quickly if not refrigerated. Therefore, canned food often doesn't work well if you have a Rat Terrier who takes hours to finish his meal. Also, most veterinarians believe that if a dog's diet consists only of canned food, he has a greater tendency to develop plaque buildup on his teeth, as well as gum disease. Studies show that dogs tend to have fewer dental problems when they eat crunchy foods that scrape against the teeth. (This does not replace regular teeth brushing and dental care.)

Semi-Moist Food

Semi-moist food can be used as an occasional treat.

Semi-moist food contains between 15 and 35 percent moisture; these products are usually shaped into beef-like bits, burgers, or whatever else dog-food company marketers think will attract the human shopper—not necessarily the dog. Most dogs are won over by the high amounts of sugar, fat, flavorings, and other chemical additives that keep the food soft. Semi-moist food is probably not the best choice for your wallet or for your dog's health. It is expensive and very high in sugar content. However, a packet of semi-moist can help you out when you are traveling, or you can use it as an occasional treat when training. Some Rat Terrier owners have found that semi-moist food can also get a finicky eater to consume his meals more readily. However, you may run the risk of a fussy eater becoming so enamored with extra-tasty semi-moist food that he doesn't want to eat anything else—a circumstance similar to a person eating candy or fast food every day. As always, check the label and evaluate semi-moist foods against the nutritional needs of your Rat Terrier.

Non-Commercial Diets

You may hear people say that they feed their Rat Terrier "non-commercial" dog food. What they mean is that they personally make their dog's food with ingredients that are not manufactured exclusively for dogs. This means that dog

Some dog owners choose to make home-cooked meals for their pets.

food that is made by a pet food company is often called commercial dog food, and dog food that is made at home by the pet owner is called non-commercial. The non-commercial diet is usually divided into two categories: cooked and raw.

Home-Cooked Diet
Some dog owners decide to make their own homemade dog food. Since 2007, when there was a large recall of tainted commercially manufactured dog food, much attention has been paid to homemade dog food. As a result, it is easier than ever to find well-balanced recipes in books and online. It is important to understand that this type of home cooking doesn't mean just giving

your dog table scraps and leftovers. The same nutritional guidelines have to be imposed upon your cooking. You will need to include the proper percentages of animal-source proteins, fats, minerals, and vitamins.

With the health of your dog so dependent upon proper nutrition, you may want to consider making his meals yourself. In a book published in 1996, *Nutrition and Care of Companion Animals*, Nancy A. Irlbeck estimated that 35 percent of all dog owners were home-cooking for their dogs. This statistic is probably much higher for today's Rat Terrier households. I surmise that the problems with commercial dog foods and associated recalls in the last few years, as well as the relatively small amount of food needed by a Rat Terrier, have encouraged more and more owners to prepare their dog's meals.

The key to the homemade diet is to stay within the nutrition guidelines for healthy dog food, as defined by the Association of American Feed Control

A raw diet consists of raw meat and vegetables, along with vitamin and mineral supplements.

A healthful diet makes for a healthy dog.

Officials (AAFCO) and to check with your vet to make sure that what you're feeding is nutritionally complete. It is easier than ever to find well-balanced recipes in books and online. Once you find one you like, review it with your vet to make sure that it is nutritionally complete. Then, when following the recipe, adhere to the ingredients list stringently; substituting or omitting ingredients often unbalances the nutritional formula. Most recipes yield large amounts that can then be divided up into portions and frozen until needed.

Raw Diet

The raw diet is a rather recent phenomenon in the world of dog feeding. This regime consists of feeding raw poultry or meat, vegetables, and fruits, with vitamin and mineral supplements added. The adherents to this type of feeding cite canine ancestry—wild dogs lived on raw meat. Many veterinarians point out that this does not necessarily mean that it was the best diet for them, and that the nutritionally balanced commercial foods available today give our dogs a better-balanced, healthier meal than that of their ancestors. Studies have also claimed that raw food carries a much higher risk of certain food-borne illnesses and parasitic infections, such as salmonella and *E. coli*. The subject is quite controversial.

No less controversial is another diet that some Rat Terrier owners swear by, called the Bones and Raw Food or Biologically Appropriate Raw Food (BARF). This diet is structured around the types of foods digested by dogs' wild ancestors and contains muscle meat, ground bones, fat, organ meats, vegetables, and fruits. Again, opponents warn repeatedly against possible dangers associated with raw foods. Many Rat Terrier owners who feed a raw diet say that their dogs have cleaner teeth, shinier coats, and fewer health problems, and that the benefits outweigh any risks. If you want to learn more about the BARF diet, many books and websites are devoted to the topic. Also, talk to your vet to see if this type of diet is right for your dog.

As your Rat Terrier ages, his diet should be adjusted to reflect his changing lifestyle.

You can check your dog's weight easily because of his short single coat.

The Senior Diet

As your Rat Terrier ages, his diet should be adjusted to reflect his changing lifestyle. An adult dog doesn't need the same amount of protein as a growing puppy. Just like a human, a dog's metabolism changes. Unless your dog is extremely active, you can reduce the protein for an adult dog to around 17 to 22 percent. A senior dog will need even less as his activity level lowers. Too much food for a less active dog can result in obesity and health issues.

As a breed, Rat Terriers age more slowly than large dogs, but somewhere between the ages of 8 and 12 years you might want to think of your furry companion as a senior citizen. As long as your dog continues to thrive, you can keep him on the same diet. Your veterinarian can give you the best advice on your individual dog. However, if you are feeding a commercial dog food and want to switch to something especially designed for an older dog, be aware that currently there are no clearly defined guidelines for senior nutrition. Foods labeled as "senior" can vary greatly from one company to the other. Some have extra protein and calories, and others are just the reverse. Therefore, the only reason to make a switch is because of your dog's health, not just his age.

Most often, elderly dogs need fewer calories as they age, but weight gain can indicate a problem like Cushing's disease, so check with your veterinarian before putting your dog on a diet. A dog with decreased kidney function needs less protein. If your dog is simply gaining too much weight, pay close attention to what he eats and how much exercise he gets. He may need to be encouraged to increase his exercise through short, gentle walks. Boost your dog's fiber intake and reduce his calories by adding canned pumpkin (plain, not pie filling) to his food. Extra pounds (kg) can lead to other health issues, such as joint stiffness and pancreatitis.

On the other hand, some dogs get

As a breed, Rat Terriers age more slowly than large dogs.

Check It Out

FEEDING CHECKLIST

Your dog needs the following basic nutrients:

- ✓ carbohydrates
- ✓ fat
- ✓ fiber
- ✓ minerals: calcium, phosphorus, magnesium, manganese, potassium, copper, sodium and chloride or chloride zinc,

chromium, sulphur, iron, selenium, cobalt, iodine
- ✓ protein
- ✓ vitamins: vitamin A, B vitamins, vitamin C, vitamin D, vitamin E, vitamin K
- ✓ water

thinner as they age. Just like weight gain, thinness can be a sign of illness, but sometimes weight loss can be caused by something as simple as tooth loss making eating more difficult, and the solution may be as minor as changing to a softer food. Your veterinarian can determine the kinds and amounts of supplements your dog may need as he ages. Your geriatric dog will appreciate familiar, comfortable routines as much or more than he did when he was younger. Keep feeding him at the times he expects, twice a day, unless your vet has advised specific changes based on his health.

Obesity

Obesity is not just a problem for older Rat Terriers—it's estimated that about one-third of the dogs in the United States are overweight. Perhaps owners with long-haired breeds can say that they didn't notice those extra pounds (kg) under all that fur. Not so for Rat Terrier owners:; you can check your dog's weight easily simply by petting him. You should be able to feel and just slightly see the outline of his ribs. When you look down, his "waist" should be visible, and when looking from the side, you should be able to see the upward curve, or tuck, of his abdomen.

An overweight dog is not a healthy dog, and it is up to you to keep him healthy. Your Rat Terrier will be only too happy to accept all of those unhealthy snacks and settle down to a sedentary lifestyle. It is up to you to keep him fit. Never give him "people food" from the table. Cut down on the carbohydrates in his treats. Most dogs are happy with vegetables if you introduce them early. Free-feeding can be a path to obesity too. This is especially true if you have a multi-dog household. It is a always good idea to supervise your dog's eating habits to keep an eye on his appetite. Finally, take him for a regular walk if he is not getting enough exercise. Rat Terriers want to be with their people, and if you are sitting on that couch, he will be only too happy to join you—walking together is a healthier bonding experience for both of you.

Toxic Foods

Most dog owners have heard that chocolate is bad for dogs, but there are many other equally toxic foods that can cause serious problems. Make sure that your does not eat any of the following foods:

- **Cake batter:** Cake batter often contains raw eggs and may contain salmonella.
- **Chocolate:** Ingestion of chocolate, and especially dark chocolate, can cause abnormal heartbeat, kidney failure, and death.
- **Grapes and raisins:** These can cause kidney failure in some dogs.
- **Macadamia nuts:** These nuts can cause a toxic reaction. Symptoms include the inability to stand, ataxia (walking wobbly), depression, vomiting, muscle tremors, fever, elevated heart rate, and sometimes fatal shock.
- **Nutmeg:** Don't let your dogs eat food seasoned with nutmeg. It can cause tremors, seizures, and central nervous system damage.
- **Onions:** High levels of onion, raw or cooked, can cause life-threatening anemia.
- **Raw bread dough:** Expanding yeast dough in your pet's stomach can be deadly. It can cause abdominal pain, vomiting, and bloat.
- **Raw eggs:** These can carry salmonella.
- **Turkey/chicken bones:** Cooked poultry bones are brittle, splinter easily, and can lodge in your dog's throat or stomach.
- **Turkey/chicken skin:** High-fat foods can be hazardous to your dog.
- **Xylitol:** This sweetener is present in products from gum to sugar-free cookies. In dogs, it can cause seizures, liver failure, and death.

Chapter
5

Grooming Your
Rat Terrier

Rat Terriers are easy dogs to groom, with their short, single coat of fine hair. This coat is unlike that of many other terriers who have a double coat (a denser outer coat to protect the dog from harsh weather and a softer undercoat that works as insulation). The Rat Terrier's single coat gives him his sleek, glossy, business-like appearance. A healthy coat should feel firm and bristle-like when you run your hand over it.

One important word on grooming: If all or parts of the grooming process are too much for you to handle, find someone to do it for you. If you do not want to check anal glands or clip nails, for example, take your dog to a veterinarian or professional groomer.

Grooming Supplies

Before you get started, you will need some basic grooming supplies:

Brushes and Combs

- Bristle brush: much like a person's hairbrush, used to brush away loose dirt
- Curry brush: hard rubber brush, used to remove dead hair
- Shedding blade: a looped tool with short teeth, used to remove dead hair
- Flea comb: a comb with small, finely spaced teeth, used to remove flea dirt or fleas

Shampoo and Conditioner

- Mild shampoo: Rat Terriers can have allergic reactions to strong or perfumed shampoos
- Mild conditioner, if needed: can aid in preventing dry skin, but be aware of possible allergies

Ear Care

- Ear cleanser: to break up wax
- Cotton balls: to wipe the dog's ear clean
- Ear powder: if prescribed by your veterinarian for mites or infections

Rat Terriers need a mild shampoo because they tend to have allergic reactions to strong or perfumed shampoos.

Ask the Expert

Pam Mills, Secretary of the Rat Terrier Club of America (RTCA), finds that her dogs only need occasional baths, but her dog's nails often need trimming. She points out that "Rats" have an oval, or semi-hare, shaped foot, so often their nails do not wear down naturally like many other breeds that have a flatter foot. She suggests that owners take their Rat Terrier to a groomer and leave him there to be bathed, have his nails done, and have the anal glands expressed. Ms. Mills believes that this grooming experience is a good way for dogs to learn that if you leave them you are coming back. She feels that these "away from home and family" grooming sessions can lessen the dog's separation anxiety if some occasion arises and you do have to leave him, such as at the veterinarian's office.

Nail Care
- Claw or guillotine trimmers: to trim nails
- Filing tools if desired: alternative tool for trimming nails
- Styptic powder or substitute, such as cornstarch or flour to stop bleeding if a nail's quick gets clipped

Dental Care
- Canine toothpaste
- Canine toothbrush

Grooming as Bonding Time
Grooming time can be pleasant for both dog and owner if you begin short grooming sessions as soon as your puppy or dog has settled into your household. Establishing a good attitude about grooming is one more time when you need to out-think your terrier. Rat Terriers want to be with their people, and what could be better than a one-on-one full-body massage? Get your dog used to being handled all over his body, as well as used to lying on either side. Stay calm and use lots of positive reinforcement to help him relax. Keep the sessions short, and take your time introducing grooming tools. You may want to begin with a grooming mitt or rubber gloves. Then try a fine-toothed flea comb to make sure that he doesn't have any parasites on board. Finally, get him used to a soft brush. (Be gentle around the head and paws because these are sensitive areas.)

Brushing
Maintaining your Rat Terrier's coat will require minimal grooming. However, Rat

PUPPY GROOMING

Rat Terrier puppies may not have a lot of hair to groom, but start brushing your pup on a regular schedule. Place your puppy on a table with a nonskid mat or surface so that he won't injure himself. Use a soft-bristle brush and make the grooming session fun. Get your puppy used to lying on either side. Get him used to the grooming tools. Trim tiny little tips off his nails. Brush his puppy teeth. You want your puppy to accept his grooming as a pleasant fact of life.

Terriers shed, and the best way to deal with the excess is to brush your dog often to remove dead hair.

How to Brush

Use a soft brush or rubber curry mitt to remove loose hair regularly. Some Rat Terrier owners like a grooming tool called a shedding blade or a hard rubber brush. Rubber kitchen gloves can work as curry mitts in a pinch. (Some vacuum cleaners come with an attachment to gently suck the dead hair off. I had one dog who seemed to like this and would present himself whenever I turned on the vacuum.) Whatever you decide to use, try to groom your dog on a daily basis, although a couple of times a week is probably more realistic—and sufficient. The more you groom, though, the less dog hair you will find clinging to your clothes and furniture.

Bathing

The Rat Terrier is basically a clean dog, but you want to keep him that way. Regular brushing will remove most of the unwanted dirt, as well as loose hair. Your Rat Terrier will only need an occasional bath, probably no more two to three times a year. Timing is often determined by a doggy roll in something unpleasant or the arrival of company who might prefer a sweet-smelling Fido. But be aware that bathing your Rat Terrier too often can lead to skin problems. Some dogs suffer from sensitive skin, and overbathing can lead to hair loss and sometimes demodicosis, a type of mange. Demodicosis is often a puppy ailment, leading some to theorize that it is associated with teething and other stresses related to puppyhood. However, it may be genetic, and it also occurs in adult dogs. If your dog develops

Grooming your Rat Terrier is a good opportunity to bond with him.

any skin problems such as redness, dryness, or itchiness, seek help from your veterinarian, who will advise you about healing salves, medicated shampoos or dips, and possible antibiotic therapy.

When you decide to bathe your Rat Terrier, keep in mind the breed's sensitive skin and select a mild soap. Check with your veterinarian and your dog's breeder for suggestions. Soaps and dips that contain commercial insecticides or deodorizing doggy colognes can cause itchiness and allergic reactions, such

as hives and swelling. Check your dog carefully for any skin irritations after bathing. Fortunately, many types of shampoos are available, and you can usually find one that works well for your individual dog's skin condition.

How to Bathe

Before you shampoo your dog, give him a thorough brushing to remove obvious dirt. Then place him on a nonslip surface in a sink, shower, or tub. Whichever location you select, it will work best if you have access to a hose attachment. Check that the water is the correct temperature. Most dogs like it lukewarm or just a tad cooler. Wet the dog's coat thoroughly, leaving his head until last. The head is the most difficult part to do on many dogs because if they look down, the water drips into their eyes, but if they look up, water is apt to roll into their noses and ear canals. Apply soap to the shoulder area first and work down the dog's back and over the rest of the body.

Your Rat Terrier's ears should be inspected and cleaned regularly.

Again, save the head until last. When you are sure that you have washed your dog completely, rinse him thoroughly. This is especially important for dogs with sensitive skin. You don't want to leave any soap residue on him that can dry and irritate his skin. Once you finish, gather your wet dog up and towel him off. During the shampoo and subsequent towel off, make sure that you have inspected all of your dog's body for bumps or cuts. You may want to apply some conditioner or even a small amount of olive oil to his coat when you finish. This will keep the coat from drying out too much, but only use a small amount or you'll end up with an oily Rat Terrier and defeat the purpose of his bath.

Bath time is also a good time to clean your dog's anal glands. I usually do this when my dog is still soapy but before I lather up his head. These glands are sacs on either side of the dog's anus, and they can collect fluid that may need to be gently expressed. Many people prefer to have their dog's groomer or veterinarian do this, but if you wish to undertake this procedure, have someone with experience show you how to do it properly.

Ear Care

Your Rat Terrier's ears should be inspected and cleaned regularly—and carefully. Ears are sensitive, and most

GROOMING AS A HEALTH CHECK

One of the best ways to keep an eye on your dog's health is through regular grooming sessions. Run your hands all over your Rat Terrier. Inspect his teeth, ears, toes, and nails. This regular inspection will make you familiar with your dog's body when he is 100 percent healthy, and you'll then be able to notice any bumps, cuts, or unusual changes. You are the first-alert system for your dog's health.

dogs are protective of them. Your dog will tolerate ear cleaning better if he learns to trust you when handling them, so check them when you are first getting him used to grooming. Reward him with treats for his good behavior during ear inspections.

When examining the ears, be aware of signs of ear disease. These include a foul odor emitting from the ear, excessive scratching or rubbing of the ear, shaking or holding the head to one side, discharge from the ear, redness or swelling in the ear canal or of the ear flap, a painful ear, or any overall behavior changes such as lack of activity or irritability. Some common reasons for ear disease, or otitis externa, might be food allergies, ear mites (only visible under a microscope), a bacterial or yeast infection, a scratch or cut, or even some foreign matter stuck in the ear. If your dog has several ear infections, your veterinarian may want to test for hypothyroidism because an imbalance of the thyroid can affect a dog's ears.

How to Care for the Ears

You can do a lot to lessen the chances of ear infections by regularly cleaning your dog's ears. Ears that become too moist are more likely to permit the growth of bacteria or yeast. Cleaning your dog's ears isn't difficult if you have trained your dog to stay still for ear inspections. Do a thorough ear cleaning during one of your weekly grooming sessions. Ask your veterinarian to suggest a good ear cleanser. Fill your dog's ear with the cleanser solution and massage the base of the ear for 30 seconds; this will help the cleanser loosen the wax inside the ear. Then wipe the ear out with a cotton ball. Do not use a cotton swab; it is too easy to poke your dog if he moves suddenly. You may need to wipe the ear a few times until the cotton comes out clean. If you clean your dog's ears regularly, yet he is still bothered by them, take him to the veterinarian. If your dog has ear mites, your veterinarian will give you a medicated ear powder to deal with them.

In general, Rat Terrier eyes require minimal grooming.

or pad which comes with dog eye cleansers. Gently wipe the cloth over the eye moving from front to back. Make sure that you only touch the outer skin around the eye and never the actual eye, which can become scratched.

If you think that your dog has excessive discharge, you should have his eyes checked by your veterinarian, as it can be a symptom of an eye problem called primary lens luxation. (See Chapter 9: Health of your Rat Terrier.) Usually this discharge simply indicates that your dog is allergic to something in his environment and the veterinarian may prescribe antibiotic eye drops or cream. One last note about eye care: Never let your dog hang his head out the car window. The fast-moving air can carry all sorts of dust and debris that might damage his eyes.

Dental Care

In addition to paying close attention to your Rat Terrier's ears and eyes, you need to learn how to care for his teeth. While most of us recognize the importance of good oral hygiene for humans, we have only recently come to understand the relationship between a dog's teeth and his overall health. Studies have linked periodontal disease to kidney, liver, and heart disease.

Eye Care

In general, Rat Terrier eyes require minimal grooming, but be sure to inspect them during a grooming session. Some mucus and crusty buildup in the corner of his eyes is normal, and you can remove it away with a clean damp cloth, tissue,

How to Care for the Teeth

First of all, make sure that you have your Rat Terrier's teeth evaluated by a veterinarian when he has his annual checkup. Most veterinarians suggest daily brushing. This is not easy to do with a dog unless he is trained to accept it. As with all other new experiences, introduce tooth brushing just like anything else—slowly, with rewards and lots of patience.

First, get your dog used to having you handle his mouth. Not all dogs welcome this, so start by dipping your finger in something that tastes good, like beef broth or even peanut butter. Be careful and go slowly. This is to get your dog used to you touching his teeth—not for you to get used to getting bitten. If you can only touch his teeth to start with, that is fine. Slow and steady wins this race.

Once you have been successful in getting your dog to allow you to handle his mouth, try wrapping your finger in gauze and rubbing his teeth and gums. It is easiest to start in the front and work back down the sides. One of the targets is the gum line, where bacteria-causing plaque lurks.

When your dog accepts this invasion into his mouth, you are ready to introduce the tools of the trade: first the toothbrush and then the toothpaste. Once you and your pet have the gauze routine down pat, it is time to introduce a toothbrush. You can choose one that is designed for dogs or use a small child's brush with soft bristles. Dog-type toothbrushes include one that is angled for a dog's mouth, a double-sided one, or finger-covering brushes that are like a plastic sleeve with bristles that fits over your finger. Brush in a gentle circular motion, paying close attention to the gum line.

Never use human toothpaste when brushing your Rat Terrier's teeth. Human

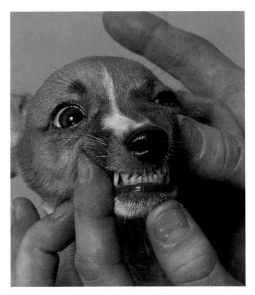

Ideally, your dog's teeth should be brushed and his mouth inspected daily.

NYLABONE

toothpaste is meant to be spit out, and no amount of dog training is going to accomplish that feat with your dog. Plus, you want to find a toothpaste that your dog likes because this will double as a treat. Some Rat Terriers prefer pastes or gels that are beef- or chicken-flavored, but others like more minty flavors. My dogs do not like those that are baking soda-based, with citrus flavors. You might save some money if you can find small samples of different flavors to test on your dogs.

In addition to brushing your dog's teeth with toothpaste, you may find many other products to help with your Rat Terrier's oral care. These include dental chews and treats, such as Nylabones, dental sprays and rinses, dental pads and sponges, dental toys, and even water additives. Dental care for dogs is a burgeoning field, so keep asking your veterinarian and reading about new products as they become available.

Nail Care

You also need to know how to trim your dog's nails. Like our fingernails, a dog's nails are constantly growing and need regular attention. The speed of nail growth can vary from dog to dog and depends on the dog's lifestyle and environment. If you walk your dog on concrete sidewalks or other hard, rough surfaces, his nails may not need to be trimmed as often as those of a dog who spends his days on grass or other soft

You will need to learn how to trim your dog's nails.

Check It Out

BASIC GROOMING

Regular grooming sessions should include:
- ✔ brushing
- ✔ cleaning of teeth
- ✔ currying or use of other   shedding

- tool
- ✔ trimming of nails
- ✔ wiping of ears

surfaces. A rough surface will act as a nail file and grind down your dog's nails naturally.

Unfortunately, my dogs spend their days running around in a grassy yard, so I have had to learn the skill of nail clipping. If, like my dogs, your Rat Terrier is mostly on grass, you will have to clip his nails as part of your regular grooming routine. If you let his nails become too long, they are likely to break and split, which can lead to infections. Some dogs are so bothered by long nails that they will alter their gait, which can cause bone damage.

How to Care for the Nails

Rat Terriers, as well as every other dog I have known, are not fond of having their nails trimmed. Start handling your dog's paws when he is young, and remember to reward him for tolerating this exercise. Once he is willing to let you hold his paws, try holding each individual nail. Keep the session short and stress free.

Use a soothing voice, and he will become accustomed to this procedure. Dispense small treats and praise as you work.

Before you actually trim your dog's nails, see if you can observe a professional groomer or veterinarian clip them. Often a professional will have several types of trimmers, so you can determine which will work best for your dog. I use the guillotine type in which the nail is slipped through a metal hoop and when the handles are closed, a metal blade slides across the hoop and slices the nail off. Another kind of clipper is the claw type, which is more like scissors except that the blades have semi-circular indentations where the nail is placed. When the handles are squeezed, the nail is cut. A third way of trimming a nail is by using an electric grinder, which is like a dremel tool. I know some people swear by this, but I have been unable to get my dogs to accept it. And frankly, I would rather cut the nails and finish the whole process quickly. Carmeta French of Warren Mountain Rat Terriers gives her dog a little treat after trimming each nail. She also uses a dremel tool after clipping the nails to round off the sharp edges. "That way, the dog's nails won't dig into into you when jumping up into your lap, which Ratties like to do LOT." Whichever nail trimming tool you select, read the directions first. Instructions for the guillotine type will explain that they must be used from below the paw so that the blade slides from the bottom to top— never the other way around.

Knowing how to cut a dog's nails is easier when you understand what a nail actually looks like inside and out. The outer protective layer is hard, but inside is a softer part with blood vessels and nerve ending; this is called the *quick*. The blood vessel shows up as pink in light-colored nails, although the quick might be hard to see in dark nails. Because you want to avoid nicking the quick, trimming light-colored nails is easier than doing dark nails. Unfortunately, most dogs seem to have dark nails, so it is difficult to see where the blood vessel and accompanying nerves extend. To trim a dark-colored nail, slice off tiny slivers rather than one piece. After each little snip, look at the clipped part of the nail. If there is a dark or pinkish spot in the middle of the newly clipped area, stop. This is

the beginning of the quick, and you don't want to cut any further. The more you trim your dog's nails, the more the quick will recede, so regular trimming will improve your dog's nail health.

Now that you understand the procedure, have your dog lie down on a raised table on which you have secured a nonslip covering or mat. It is a good idea to have someone help hold your dog the first time you undertake nail trimming because you need the pup to be stationary when you make the clip. Get the tool in the right spot and squeeze the handle. A sliver of nail should drop off. The goal in nail clipping is to remove enough of the nail

See which type of nail trimmer works best for your dog.

so that, when the dog is standing, his nail does not touch the ground. A good rule of thumb is that when you hear the click-clack of nails on the floor as your dog approaches, it is time to bring out the nail clippers.

Don't forget that if your Rat Terrier has dewclaws, these need to be clipped too. The dewclaw is an extra claw that grows partway up on the inside of the dog's leg. Not all Rat Terriers have dewclaws. The breed standard does not permit them on the forelegs and encourages their removal from the hind legs because dewclaws can snag on things and rip off. If you have a dog with dewclaws, trim them regularly so that they do not become so long that they curl. Once the nails are done, check the dog's pads. Make sure that no foreign objects are stuck between the pads.

One last word about nails: People who have been trimming nails for years occasionally cut the quick. Even in experienced hands, a dog can wiggle just at the wrong moment. Clipping the quick hurts, and most dogs yelp. To make matters worse, the nail will bleed a fair amount. The best way to deal with this is to stay calm so that your dog doesn't become any more distressed. Remember, this is a sensitive spot, and your dog may react as if you have amputated his paw, but don't panic—it is not dire. You just have to be vigilant that the cut does not become dirty and infected.

Before beginning nail trimming, purchase some styptic powder or a styptic stick to use to promote clotting and stop the flow of blood from a dog's broken nail. If you can't find styptic powder, use cornstarch or flour. Don't let the dog walk off on his own for a while, because he can reopen the cut by walking around or licking it. When the bleeding lessens, use a clean paper towel or tissue to apply some pressure to the nail. Later, after the bleeding has finished, wash and bandage the paw so that it is kept clean. Have your veterinarian check the nail to prevent infection.

Training Your
Rat Terrier

A bored, restless Rat Terrier is not a happy Rat Terrier—nor is his owner happy. However, the good news is that a Rat Terrier is one of the most readily trained dog breeds. Like most dogs, he wants a job to expend energy and stimulate his mind. It is up to you to write out the job description.

Why Training Is Important

Training is one of the best things you can do to improve the quality of your dog's life. A trained dog is can go places and meet people. When people come to your home, your Rat Terrier will not have to be shut away in another room because he is yapping or jumping on them. He can be a well-mannered participant in the party, and few things make Rat Terriers happier than being in the middle of everything. A dog who can walk quietly on a leash, come when called, sit, lie down, and stay when instructed is a dog who can be trusted, and therefore, he can be given more freedom. In addition, these basic commands can sometimes save your dog's life; you may need him to come or to drop into a *down* position immediately in a dangerous situation.

Positive Training

Dogs learn better when they are not intimidated or fearful. Training must be a happy experience where the dog can make a mistake and not be terrified of repercussions. Your dog will respond well to verbal praise and to treats. The hallmark of positive training is that the trainer labels the desired behavior with a word, such as "come" and rewards the pup when he demonstrates the behavior. Unwanted behavior is either ignored or the trainer refuses to interact with the dog. Positive training works extremely well with Rat Terriers because most seem to love learning new things and hate being ignored by their people.

Treats are used to reinforce good behavior, and they are given as soon as the dog does what you have asked him to do. Treats should be small and something the dog likes. You want the treat to be about the size of a large vitamin pill so that he can "wolf it down" quickly. You don't want to pause your training so that he can chew for 30 seconds. Also, it is a good idea to have a variety of treats.

Positive training uses treats and praise to reinforce good behavior.

FINDING A TRAINER

Dog training has evolved from punishment for negative actions to positive reinforcement for positive actions. In general, this works well for all dogs. However, you must be aware that dogs are dogs, and we cannot always think the way they do. If there is some behavior that can be dangerous to the dog (chasing cars, not coming when he is called) or to people (snapping, biting), do not hesitate to get help. Find a trainer or obedience class where you will learn how to deal with this behavior effectively. One resource is the Association of Pet Dog Trainers (APDT) (www.apdt.com).

You might want to use lower-value treats, such as small kibble pieces or a piece of sugar-free cereal, and move up the flavor spectrum to bits of cheese (string cheese works well) to pieces of hot dogs. It is tempting to give just the lower-value treats to reinforce tricks the dog has already mastered, but this can make the dog lose interest in those exercises. Mixing up the treats works best. When you are working with your dog, watch him take his treats:

Kibble, kibble, kibble, hot dog. "Wait a minute, was that a hot dog? Hot dog!" Your dog will perk right up and respect his surprising handler a little more. Finally, as you progress, you will wean him off regular treats. If you show your dog in obedience, you will not be permitted to use any treats in the show ring. Also, just in general, you want to make sure that your dog will work for your praise alone. Give your dog lots of verbal praise and petting. Lucky for you, you are with a Rat Terrier and basically all he wants to do is please you.

Finally, while you are using treats, you don't want to work with your dog just after he has eaten. Would you want to work for food when you had just had a full meal? Also, estimate the amount of treats you dole out. Active puppies can seem to eat endlessly without gaining weight, but as your dog matures, adjust the size of his meals to accommodate the amount of treats he is receiving.

Socialization

In the broadest terms, canine socialization means training your dog how to interact with people, animals, and the elements of his environment (such as garbage trucks, elevators, and sirens).

Socialization means training your dog to accept different people, animals, and situations.

When you socialize your dog, you need to introduce him to as many different experiences as possible so that he can learn how to respond reasonably to unfamiliar things. Dogs are wired to be part of a pack and to be protective of that group. Therefore, new people and places can bring out a defensive or an attack reaction. Socialization means that you teach your dog to make proper (by human standards) responses.

Carmeta French of Warren Mountain Rat Terriers says that socialization is a must for all of her dogs, from puppies to adults. She notes that it is important to be sure that a puppy does not catch any sicknesses while out and about, so she recommends that Ratties meet several vaccinated, healthy, and well-behaved dogs before they hit 12 weeks of age. Also, he should meet any other animals that the dog may have to live with, such as cats and birds that must be respected as members of the family. Most dogs will respect these other animals if they have the law laid down early enough. However, if a cat or other animal is not familiar to that dog, he may go after it.

Carmeta continues to say that the dog should meet many people, big, small, old, young, different smells (perfumes, different outfits, etc.). She had a Rat

Terrier freak out when he met a guy who wore too much stinky cologne. The pup had never smelled such a thing and this was just too much. Dog's noses are sensitive, but they need to learn to associate all smells (even unpleasant ones) with people, who hand out treats and affection. With a little work and lots of experiences, Ratties will learn to like everybody and everything.

Crate Training

When you get a dog, you will want to give him a room of his own—a crate. The crate aids in housetraining (see section below), but it also serves as his safe haven in many locations: at home, in the car, and in a motel or someone else's house. Don't let anyone, including children, bother your dog when he is in his crate. The dog has every right to feel that this is a place of his own where he can be calm. If people tease him when he is confined, he might become overly protective of his space. Most puppies and dogs like their crates because it appeals to their ancestral need for a den, but some have to get used to being confined. In those cases, training your dog to stay in a crate requires time and patience.

First, your crate needs to be the correct size for your dog. (See Chapter 3: Supplies.) Place the crate in an area where your Rat Terrier will feel like he is part of the family. He won't want to be stuck in the basement or laundry room when everyone else is in the kitchen, and he may complain by barking and fussing. I like to use a crate that is portable enough so that I can move it around the house as needed. At night, it comes into the bedroom. Even a fairly young puppy can soon learn that we all settle down then.

Other than nighttime, don't leave your dog in a crate for long periods. The crate is not a jail sentence; it is a safe place for his quiet time. It is also a place to leave your Rat Terrier when you are away from home. But keep the confinement times as short as possible, especially with a young dog. You want him to be fond of his crate, and you defeat this purpose if he is left in

it too long.

If your dog does complain about being left in is crate, never take him out of it when he is fussing or barking. This will just reinforce the noisy behavior. Wait until he has stopped for a few minutes and then welcome him out while giving him lots of praise. Another way to keep him happy during his short times of confinement is to drop in an occasional treat and tell him what a good dog he is for being calm and quiet.

Not everyone embraces the idea of crate training because they have seen too many people who misuse it by leaving their dog in it for hours. An adult dog should not be left in a crate for more than three to four hours and a puppy much less.

Housetraining

Small dogs and terriers have a reputation for being difficult to housetrain, so you have a dual challenge with your Rat Terrier. However, with some wise choices and persistence, you should be able to surmount any obstacles that stand in your way.

How to Housetrain

The first thing you need for housetraining is a crate. The crate needs to be large enough for your dog to stand, sit, and turn around in comfortably. The crate is your Rat Terrier's den and a place he will not want to soil. This innate wish to keep his sleeping area clean is your best tool in housetraining your dog. When you can't supervise him for a short period, place him in his crate. As soon as you release him from the crate, give him a chance to relieve himself.

Pay attention to the signals he gives when he needs to eliminate. Usually, a dog will sniff the ground, sometimes in a circular motion. If he is about to go, clap your hands to get his attention and distract him. Quickly take him outside. Praise him for going in the right spot.

Take your puppy outside to potty when he finishes eating, napping, or playing.

Puppy Love

PUPPY CLASS

If you are fortunate enough to find an obedience school that offers puppy classes, go and observe one. Most classes will not accept puppies until they have had all of their vaccinations at 12 to 16 weeks of age. Puppy classes usually cover the basic commands that you have already been teaching, but they also provide something else—a chance to meet and interact with other puppies and responsible dog owners who, like you, are interested in making the effort to raise a dog who will be a good companion. Puppy class is a great place for you to socialize your Rat Terrier.

(Don't forget that you need to clean up after your pet in any public place.)

Many owners of small dogs decide to train their dogs to use indoor "piddle pads," rather than an outdoor potty area. These pads are available at most pet supply stores. They measure about 20 by 22 inches (51 by 56 cm) and have been treated with a special scent to encourage the dog to eliminate on them. The pads have a waterproof backing to protect your floors, and they also come with a tray. Usually, the pad is placed near the door so that once a dog has learned to use it, you can easily move the pad outside and complete outdoor training if you wish. The pads can be handy if you live in an apartment or in a cold climate, and you're reluctant to go outside when your dog needs to eliminate first thing in the morning and last thing in the evening.

Take your puppy to his piddle pad or outside elimination area when he finishes eating, napping, or playing. Until he is fully trained, you must be with your dog. This is important so that you can teach him a word such as "potty" to associate with elimination. Every time he "performs," use the word and praise him. If he does not go potty right away, wait five to ten minutes and take him inside. In another five to ten minutes, go back outside or put him on the pad. Like all training, this will take time and patience, but Rat Terriers are smart. If you are consistent, he will eventually get it. If you want, reward him with a small treat too.

Basic Obedience Training

No matter what you have planned for your Rat Terrier's future endeavors, basic training should include significant socialization and should begin early. Every dog should be a companion, and he

BASIC OBEDIENCE COMMANDS

Your Rat Terrier will become a confident and happy canine citizen if he is socialized early and learns early and some basic commands, such as:

✔ sit   ✔ come   ✔ stay   ✔ down   ✔ heel

should learn basic obedience commands such as *sit*, *stay*, *down*, *come*, and walk or *heel*. Rat Terriers are apt pupils and learn quickly. Pups can begin to learn simple commands when they are just seven weeks old. Even though this age is too young for formal training classes, you should give your puppy a head start with a little homeschooling.

Good training is a reflection of a good trainer, and every good trainer practices the three C's: (1) Communication: Confidently deliver clear commands; (2) Consistency: Use the same commands for the same actions; and (3) Commendation: Reward the behavior you want and ignore what you do not want to reinforce. Other letters you should add into that mix are "K" for kindness and "P" for patience and persistence—your Rat Terrier will be trying hard to figure out how to please you, so you need to be kind, patient, and persistent with him. Never correct your dog with anger when you are working with a Rat Terrier. They are tough but

sensitive little dogs. And finally, don't forget "F" for fun—training your dog is how you and he bond, and it should be fun, so enjoy it!

Sit

The *sit* will probably be the first and easiest command for your Rat Terrier pup to master. Put aside two or three short blocks of time each day to work with him. At first, you will only need about five minutes for each session, but as you progress and your dog matures, you may want to extend the times to 15 minutes. When introducing any new exercise, find a quiet spot where you and your pup can concentrate on the business at hand. You both need to put on your "working gear"—for your Rat Terrier, that means a collar or harness and lead. Your gear requires something to hold small treats that your pup really likes. You can simply put a handful of treats in a plastic baggy in your pocket, or you can attach a small "bait bag" to your belt.

How to Teach *Sit*

1. Begin with your puppy facing you. Show him the treat.
2. Hold the treat in front of his nose and gradually move it up and back over his head. Don't raise it much higher than the tip of his ears—you don't want him thinking that he has to jump for it.
3. To follow the treat, he will shift his weight onto his haunches and into a sit.
4. As soon as he sits, say "Yes!" and give him the treat.
5. After a few practices, you can add the word "sit" as a command. Practice this three or four times in one session.

He needs to figure it out and associate the word "sit" with the action.

It will take a lot of patience and repetition before your puppy makes the connection between a command word and the action you want him to perform. After all, he's learning a new language, and it will take some time for him to realize that some of the gibberish he hears humans say all day has a nugget of meaning in it just for him. If you are really paying attention, you might be lucky enough to see that moment when the light bulb goes on in your Rat Terrier's mind. In education, we call it an "Ah-ha" moment when the student gets it—perhaps it's

The *sit* command is easy for most dogs to learn.

more of an "I got it! So now where's the treat?" moment for your puppy.

Come

The *come* command is probably the most important command your dog will learn. If he escapes from his yard or breaks free from his leash, you should be able to call him back quickly. Fortunately, this command is easy for your Rat Terrier. One thing he wants to do is to be with you— and even more so if you have some treats. For this important command to work, you don't want your dog to have any negative connotations about the word "come." NEVER use it when you want your dog to come for something unpleasant, such as grooming or a nail trim.

How to Teach *Come*

1. When your dog is a little distance away from you and not paying attention to what you are doing, call his name and say "Come!" He will probably come right away, so reward him with a treat.
2. Do this whenever you can throughout the day. Be sure to reward him with a treat each time. Soon your Rat Terrier will understand that when you use the word "come," you can be relied upon for a treat.

You can see how well your Rat Terrier understands the *come* command by involving your family and friends in the "learning game." With two or three people armed with treats, take turns calling your dog from one person to the other. Reward him whenever he comes.

Stay

The *stay* command is almost as important as the *come* command when it comes to your dog's safety. You can use it if there is a situation when you need your dog to remain still in one place for a period. I found out the value of this one day when a guest dropped a crystal bowl (a dog show trophy) in my kitchen one day. It shattered into a gazillion shards and my dog was standing in the midst of it. A crisp *stay* kept him frozen in place until I could pick him up and remove him from the situation.

How to Teach *Stay*

1. Have your dog sit (or you can do this when he is in a *down*). Reward him.
2. Then stand up and calmly say "Stay." Hold the palm of your hand out toward the dog as if you are signaling for him to stop.
3. If he stays for just a few seconds, return, tell him "Good stay," and reward him while he is still sitting.
4. Repeat the exercise two or three times. If he gets up, put him back into a *sit* and begin again. Once your pup understands that he is to stay in that position, you can back up a few more

inches (cm).

5. Finish by releasing your dog with a clear command. You want your dog to stay until you tell him that he can go. Lighten your voice and say "All done" or whatever cue you have chosen to show that the exercise is over.

Down

I use the *down* command for "lie down" exclusively. (If I want the dog to get off the couch, I use the command "*off*." In fact, if my dogs hear "down" when they are lying on the couch, they think that I have just told them to snuggle in for a long nap!) The *down* command is important when you want your dog to stay is one spot for a period. It is unreasonable to tell a dog to sit for a long time; tell him to lie down instead.

The *down* is a good command to establish early. Sometimes the adolescent or insecure older dog can struggle while learning to down because he might feel threatened by being ordered into such a submissive

The *down* command is important when you want your dog to stay in one spot for a period.

position. If you are working with a dog who resists the "down," continue to practice using the three C's with kindness, persistence, and patience. If you become frustrated, stop and try again later, when you can approach the lesson with a fresh and happy demeanor.

How to Teach *Down*

1. Begin with your Rat Terrier in front of you. If he already knows the *sit*, place him in a *sit*. Show him a treat.
2. Hold the treat in front of his nose. Move it down toward the floor and pull it along the floor toward you. This should look kind of like drawing an "L" shape.
3. When your pup follows the treat, he will move his head down and then out along the floor into a prone position.
4. When he is lying down, give him the treat and praise him. Stroke his back encouragingly while he is down to reinforce the behavior. Make sure that he understands that he should stay down while he receives the treat and praise. You want him to remain in that position until you release him with a command, such as "All done." Practice this three or four times in a session.

Heel

Every dog should learn to walk on a lead without pulling or tripping their accompanying human. Even if your Rat Terrier is lucky enough to have a backyard for all of his exercise, he still needs to understand that when he is told to heel he must walk quietly by your side. At the very least, this will make trips to the veterinarian easier.

How to Teach *Heel*

1. Begin with your Rat Terrier sitting next to you on your left side. (Either side will work, but because you are beginning, it makes sense to start with the side you will use if you decide to continue on to do rally or obedience work.)
2. The leash should be folded up in your right hand with just your thumb poked through the end of the loop. Your left hand should free to pat your dog or to gather up the slack from the leash if you wish.
3. When you are ready to walk forward, say your dog's name in a light, encouraging tone followed by the word "heel," and step forward with your left foot. The name will alert your dog to pay attention, and your nearby leg swinging forward will signal to him that you are walking.
4. For the first few times, your dog may have no idea what you want him to do, but when he finally moves forward, reward him enthusiastically. You will probably have to do this

The *heel* command teaches your dog to walk by your left side.

several times before he has his "Ah-ha" moment.

5. Once he understands that the "Fido, heel" means forward movement, take it a few steps further. When you are out for a formal walk that involves heeling (this is different from those walks when you expect him to sniff around and do his business), you want your dog to position himself near your left leg. This takes lots of practice, so don't expect your dog

to figure it out for quite a while. You have an advantage, though, with your Rat Terrier because his mind has him programmed to want to be with you—his favorite person.

6. Once he responds to the *heel* command, start walking and he should join you. If he lags, give a very gentle tug on his leash. Stop tugging the moment he is in the right position at your leg and praise him.

Basic Obedience Class

Think about obedience class as school for your dog. For your dog, understanding basic commands is almost as important as your children learning how to read. The world will become an easier place for your Rat Terrier to navigate with some learning. Not all schools and not all obedience classes are equal, and it is worth your time to find the best one for your Rat Terrier. Ask friends with dogs about their dog training experiences.

Anyone who has a Rat Terrier whom you think is a pleasant companion dog is a good resource. You can also explore online. One resource is the Association of Pet Dog Trainers (APDT), with their website at www.apdt.com. When you have found several likely places to train, visit some classes as an observer. Pay attention to how trainers deal with the smaller and mid-sized breeds.

After class, request to speak to the trainer. You want to know how much

Basic obedience class will make the world an easier place to navigate for your Rat Terrier.

Ask the Expert

VOICE COMMANDS

Kay Blair has been teaching obedience classes for 40 years in northern Virginia, and she shared some thoughts on training. She says that if your dog is in a dangerous situation, your voice command may just save his life. She knows what she is talking about. A graduate of her class had a dog twist out of his collar and race across a road. The frantic owner yelled, "Come" and the dog turned to run back across the road to her, but a car was coming. Before the dog stepped off the curb, the owner shouted, "Stay." The dog froze in place. The car passed and she reached him safely. Dog obedience is not just for dog shows!

experience your prospective trainer has with Rat Terriers and similar breeds. Finding someone who works wonders with a class full of German Shepherd Dogs or Border Collies but who has not trained Rat Terriers may not be the best trainer for you. This is especially important if you are training your first Rat Terrier.

Classes are great for socializing and learning, but the only way you will train your Rat Terrier is by practicing together each day. Commit to doing your homework. Carve out one or two short blocks of time to work on what is being taught in class. Most basic classes run for six to eight weeks, and many instruct you and your dog in the basic skills necessary to make your dog a good canine citizen.

If you want to see how well you are doing, you can ask your instructor about earning the American Kennel Club Canine Good Citizen (CGC) certificate.

Solving
Problems With
Your Rat Terrier

Dogs of all types can present some challenges even in the best homes and most loving environments. They are, after all, dogs, and no matter how much we attempt to humanize them, they see the world through canine eyes. People who head successful dog households are good at understanding the dog's point of view and at clarifying acceptable dog behavior versus problem behavior. Your Rat Terrier needs your guidance to become the best dog for your household.

Aggression

Aggressive behavior can manifest itself in several forms, such as snarling, growling, or even snapping.

How to Manage Aggression

One of the best ways to handle unwanted aggressive behavior is to establish yourself as "top dog" in a nonconfrontational way. If your dog is aggressive, the key to your success in changing his behavior is to show him it that it benefits him to mend his ways. Terriers have been bred to hang

Sometimes it takes a professional to solve a problem behavior.

Ask the Expert

BAD DOG?

Bad dog? Maybe, maybe not. Before you try to solve a problem with your dog, ask yourself if you really have one. Jack Ward, who ran Capital City Dog Training in northern Virginia for many years, would begin his training sessions by asking the handlers to define the problems they were having with their dogs. Often someone replied, "Mine is a bad dog because he gets on the furniture, he sleeps in my bed, and he bothers us when we are eating." Jack would then push harder and ask how the behavior started. The response was usually that the handler let the dog do all of these things when he was just a puppy and it was so-o-o cute. Jack informed the handler that she didn't have a bad dog at all; she had a good one who had learned just what they taught him. The moral to this story is: Don't teach your puppy anything you don't want him to do when he is an adult.

on when things get tough, so you don't want to go head-to-head over some issue. Your job is to outthink him and figure out some way to convince him that there is a more attractive alternative out there.

Never reward a puppy or dog for behavior that seems remotely aggressive. Growling in a young puppy isn't cute, but if you severely or physically punish him for it, you are apt to scare him into the next, and more serious, behavior. With a terrier, physical punishment almost always escalates the problem.

If your dog continues to growl or exhibit other aggressive behavior, consult a professional dog trainer immediately. The earlier you learn how to snuff out this behavior, the better your chance of thoroughly extinguishing it.

Barking (Excessive)

Barking can be a problem with some dogs—including Rat Terriers. Although most of us want a dog to bark and alert us when someone approaches our residence, no one wants a yappy little dog. The more you understand your dog, the better able you will be to shape his behavior. Remember, a Rat Terrier is genetically engineered to react if something rustles, moves, or squeaks. If you think that you have an overly vocal Rat Terrier, first examine the situations that set him off. If he is alarm barking, he is letting you and anyone within hearing distance know that something is disturbing him. Often a dog will do this sort of alarm barking near what he considers his home turf—his home, his yard, his automobile, and his people. When he is in full alarm bark mode, he is worried, and this barking is his way of dealing with the situation. Because he is a terrier, he has the determination to see things through to their logical (or at least, logical to his doggy mind) conclusion. Often, the more frantically he is told to cease, the more upset he will become, and thus the more he will bark. Talk about a vicious—and noisy—circle.

How to Manage Barking

Observe your Rat Terrier when he starts this type of alarm barking. This is not something that he enjoys; he is stressed out about some situation. He doesn't know what to do, so he is running around yelping. What he needs is to learn an alternative and acceptable behavior when he feels alarmed. You need to train him to sit or to go to his special "place" as a substitute for his barking.

The *place* command works well for dogs who become so excited that they don't know what to do. Most dogs are quick to learn that "go to your place" means that good things happen there. Give your dog a treat when he goes there on his own as well as when you put him there. The idea is that his place is a safe, pleasurable, and treat-filled area—not a location to be associated with punishment. You may think of it as the "time-out spot" parents often have for children —something children will learn to avoid. Your dog's spot should be just the opposite. It should be a place he wants to go to

A well-behaved dog will be a welcome addition to any family.

for treats and praise. Eventually, he will go there because it feels safe when he is stressed.

I usually permit two barks before I give the command, "No bark" and reward him with a treat for ceasing. After that, I tell him to go to his place and give him another treat once he is there. From this location, he can sit and watch whatever interaction takes place at the door. This behavior modification needs to be started early and takes lots of repetition. I have a jar of my dog's favorite treats on a table near the door.

Remember that your dog wants to succeed and to be rewarded. Never enter into any sort of play behavior when he is barking—that is too much of a reward. Only praise him when he quiet. You will need to go slowly and spend a lot of time training with a Rat Terrier who is a barker. While working with my worst offender, I admit to moments of despair. But I decided that my human patience (and brain) was going to outlast his dogged determination. In the end, I think it was the treats—and long-suffering friends who would stand patiently on the other side of the door or come in and go back out until my dogs were in their "places."

This same sort of barking can be a problem if you are taking your dog on a walk and he insists on yapping at every person or animal along the way. Take along treats and tell him to sit whenever something alarms him. Treat him and keep him sitting until whatever alarmed him has passed by. This will take practice, so be sure to pack your patience along with his treat bag. The more relaxed and matter-of-fact you are on the walk, the more your dog will settle down. If he feels you tense up when a dog is approaching, you are signaling that there is something to be alarmed about. It also helps to use the walk itself as a reward. If your dog loves his walks, you can abruptly turn around and go home whenever he starts barking. Always remember that your dog is studying your behavior even more closely than you are watching his. Rat Terriers are smart, and if they want to go on those walks, they will pretty soon pick up on what behavior is acceptable on an outing. The key is patience and consistent positive reinforcement. No dog wants to fail—yours is trying to figure out how to please you.

Chewing

Chewing is another problem that often results from lack of exercise and boredom. However, you must be aware that there is a difference between a puppy's chewing and an adult dog's chewing. Puppies chew for two primary reasons: They are learning about the world the way dogs do—with their mouths; or they are teething, and chewing eases painful gums. Puppies need items to

PUPPIES AREN'T PEOPLE

One thing to remember when you are working with a puppy is that he is trying his very best to please you. He has to sort through all of his canine instincts and adapt them to fit into your world as best he can. Don't make the mistake of attributing human feelings to him. You will probably hear someone say that her dog misbehaved because he was mad at her. Does this owner really think that her dog stays home just conjuring up ways to get revenge for some slight done to him? It is more likely that the dog was simply bored, and the fluffy pillow was just sitting there waiting to be unstuffed. Nor is a puppy who hangs his head when you scold him admitting guilt. Animal behaviorists say that the "guilty look" is simply a submissive posture. He is responding to the tone of your voice, which tells him that you are angry about something. You can pamper your puppy as much as you like, but you will train him better if you remember that he is first and last a canine.

chew, and it is up to you to provide them with chewable toys, such as Nylabones, and you are equally responsible for removing everything that they shouldn't chew from their environment when they are not supervised. These items include some canine favorites: gloves, shoes, books, and all dangerous items such as electrical cords. Also, never give your puppy something similar to what he should not chew. For example, don't give him an old shoe and expect him to differentiate between a worn-out shoe and a brand-new one.

An adult Rat Terrier may also chew, and this can be very destructive. Some of the common reasons why he is still chewing as an adult are that he was not taught "chewing rules" as a puppy, he is not receiving enough stimulation, or he is anxious or fearful. Give your dog toys that he can chew, and praise him for his selection of appropriate items. Note that Rat Terriers can be tough on toys. Most tend to "kill" any new offering. Supervise your dog to see how serious he is about destroying toys. My dogs cannot be trusted with anything that squeaks—they go straight for that noisemaker, and I don't want them swallowing it. Stuffed toys are short-lived, too, because Rat Terriers can rip them open and spread around every fiber of the filling in a few seconds. The dogs seem to enjoy this exercise, but I always end up retrieving stuffing because I don't want them to choke on it. While doing this, I ponder why I spend good money on a toy that lasts only a few minutes. My dogs do best with hard rubber toys that can be filled with treats.

Remember that all dogs need supervision when they are playing with toys. A small chunk of anything can cause choking.

How to Manage Chewing

If your dog is destroying things with excessive chewing, examine the amount of exercise and "people time" he is getting. Remember, your dog is not trying to punish you by ripping up your favorite book; he is occupying himself because he is bored or stressed. Rat Terriers need both physical and mental stimulation with their people to become the wonderful little companion dogs they can be.

To keep the no-chew policy on track, try applying a bitter-tasting, dog-repellant spray to things like furniture legs that you want to keep canine tooth-free. However, experiment with these commercially available sprays: One of my dogs seems to think that bitter taste is a nice seasoning for table legs. Even if your dog doesn't like the

If house soiling is a problem with your Rat Terrier, teach him that cleanliness is a desirable thing.

FINDING A DOG TRAINER

The Association of Pet Dog Trainers (APDT) (www.apdt.com) has declared January as "National Train Your Dog" month, so maybe a good New Year's resolution would be to locate a trainer for any problems you might be having with your Rat Terrier. Some behaviors that you want to extinguish can often been dealt with in obedience classes. Ask your veterinarian and dog-owning friends, or visit the APDT on the Internet to find the names of obedience schools in your region. Interview the trainers and be honest with the problems you wish to correct. Listen to the trainer if she suggests a multi-pronged approach. One of the biggest reasons for dog misbehavior is that the dog has too much canine energy and too much time on his paws. Your trainer may suggest activities such as agility to burn off some excess energy.

---

spray taste at first, the taste wears off quickly, so you'll need to reapply frequently.

Another word of warning to help you with a chewer: Avoid chasing your dog when he has something in his mouth that you don't want him to have. When you do this, you've just about shouted "Game time!" and you have rewarded him with your attention. Your dog will love the chase game and only want to repeat this attention-getting behavior. The best way to get the item is to call your dog to you calmly, tell him to sit, and give him a treat. You can nonchalantly pick up the article while he is eating his treat.

Digging

Rat Terriers dig for a variety of reasons. First of all, they are terriers, and terriers are genetically programmed to "go to ground." The second reason is that digging is fun for most dogs. They may also have a legitimate terrier reason for this behavior, such as chasing down rodents, burying toys or food, finding cool spots to lie down in, or escaping under a fence.

How to Manage Digging

You need to outfox your digger, but this may require some diligent work. Sometimes dogs can be distracted from digging by giving them increased exercise and more engaging toys. Another tactic is to set up a special place where digging is allowed. When you catch your dog digging in your favorite flower bed, tell him "No" and move him to "his" digging spot. Then give him a command such as "Okay, dig." Praise him when he digs in the right place. To make this acceptable digging spot inviting, you might want to mix sand into the dirt to loosen it. If he still doesn't get the idea, mine the soil with a favorite toy or some yummy treats.

House Soiling

Most Rat Terriers are easy to housetrain, but some can be difficult and others can slide back into poor habits. Examine some of the common probable causes to find a fix:

- illness—always check with your veterinarian whenever there is a change in your dog's behavior
- change in food
- change in schedule
- stress—especially when left alone
- no one understands or is watching for the dog's signals that he needs to go outside
- scent marking—occurs more often in multiple pet households and with unneutered males

Rat Terriers have more of a propensity to dig than some other breeds.

PROBLEM BEHAVIORS CHECKLIST

Every dog owner should be aware of the signs of an aggressive dog. See a trainer if your dog develops any of the following behaviors. Keep your dog away from other dogs who exhibit them:

- ✓ excessive and "nasty" barking
- ✓ snarling, growling, or snapping (even if it is to protect food, it is not a good sign)
- ✓ overguarding of possessions from other pets and people
- ✓ fearfulness in new situations or around strangers (fear is the leading cause of dog bites)
- ✓ severe attacks on other animals, such as cats or livestock
- ✓ snapping and snarling when petted, groomed, or lifted
- ✓ chasing moving objects such as bicycles, skateboards, cars, and trucks

How to Manage House Soiling

If you have an older dog who came from another environment and house soiling is an issue, you may have to begin housetraining as if he were a puppy. (See Chapter 6: Training Your Rat Terrier.) Housetraining is based on a dog's instinctive desire to eliminate away from his "nest" area. This can be challenging if the dog was raised in dirty conditions and doesn't appreciate the difference between clean and soiled bedding. This often occurs if puppies are kept in a barn or box where all the floor space is covered with straw or shavings. Once they have learned not to care, it can be difficult to reteach them. It can be done, however, with persistence and patience. But you'll have to start at square one, as if he were a puppy.

Teach your dog that cleanliness is a desirable thing. Keep his bedding clean. If your dog doesn't know how to keep his bed clean, construct his bedding of towels or other easily washed items. Pick them up and wash them often.

Also, put your dog on a schedule and stick to it. Some house soiling issues are caused by owners who leave their dogs alone for long stretches of time. The ability to "hold it" changes as a dog ages. Puppies and older dogs need to eliminate more often than those in the prime of life. However, no dog should be expected to housetrain himself if no one is around. When you are away for long periods, find a dog walker for your pet.

Go out with your dog and praise him when he eliminates. House soiling problems and regression to house soiling sometimes occurs when the dog is simply put outside alone. If you have a nice, safe backyard, it can be tempting to just let the dog out. However, this doesn't work with a dog who is having house soiling issues. You need to go out with him and praise him for eliminating in the proper location. And yes, that means on rainy or snowy mornings too.

Another problem occurs when a dog has not learned how to alert his owner when he needs to go outside. You need to learn your dog's signs, and you need to make it clear to your dog that you get the signal. Use a word such as "out" every time he does the behavior, and take him outside.

If your dog is small enough to be picked up, don't always automatically pick him up when your "time to take the dog out" schedule dictates. If you do, you may find that your dog doesn't have any idea of how to alert you that he needs to go out. What he *has* learned is that some marvelous hands swoop down and take him outside periodically. I have one friend who found out this was the problem with her dog. She finally hung a little bell on the wall near the door and whenever she was ready to take the dog out, she rang the bell and said "Out." The dog caught on fast and rang the bell whenever he wanted an outing.

Jumping Up

I love dogs, but that does not mean that I like being jumped on—especially when I am dressed in either good clothes or shorts. Nondog lovers certainly don't appreciate those sharp little nails digging into their clothes and legs. A responsible dog owner will discourage jumping up on anyone.

How to Manage Jumping Up

Someone once told me that a dog wants to "be in your face," and from the dog's point of view, the rest of your body is just an obstacle to this nose-to-nose contact. If your Rat Terrier seems to have springs instead of legs, examine what sets off the behavior and direct him to an appropriate alternative behavior. Common triggers for jumpers are your arrival home, a friend's arrival, meal time, and walk time. To add to the dog's confusion about jumping in my house, not all of the family members were consistent in their reactions to being jumped on. Therefore, we had to develop a few specific commands related to jumping.

First, give the action a simple name. We selected the word "jump." Our dog is allowed to jump when given that command. He is not allowed to jump when given the command "No ups." We dropped the word "jump" from the *no* command to avoid confusion. When he starts to bounce around, we tell him "No up," then tell him to go to his place. He is rewarded once he is in his place and told to sit and wait. This behavior is covered in basic obedience training (see Chapter 6: Training Your Rat Terrier), which is strongly suggested for a well-behaved Rat Terrier.

One further note about jumping: Make sure that your dog gets lots of exercise. If your Rat Terrier is so energetic that he

For many dogs, jumping up is a natural behavior.

cannot stand still long enough for his brain to process "no ups," you need to examine if he is getting enough exercise.

Nipping

Nipping is often associated with "mouthy" dogs who like to chew, but it can also be a sign of aggression. A puppy's mother and littermates are usually the first tutors in teaching him not to nip. If you have a chance, watch a group of puppies and their mother interact. Often a mother or littermate who is nipped too hard will yelp and stop playing with the little nipper. This lesson is important to all puppies and can sometimes be missed when a puppy is removed from his canine family too early; it's one reason why puppies should stay with their mother and littermates until at least eight weeks of age. One way to correct nipping behavior is to model your teaching behavior on that of a mother dog's.

How to Manage Nipping

First, don't use your fingers or toes as playthings with a young pup. That is just setting your dog up for a problem. Any time you pet your puppy and he nips your fingers, yell something like "Ow!" or "Ouch!" Make enough of a fuss so that you get his attention and he stops playing. Rat Terriers are smart and sensitive dogs; if you do this every time (no exceptions), they will pick up on your displeasure

A well-trained dog will be less likely to exhibit problem behaviors.

If you continue to have trouble with nipping, continue to say "Ow!" when he does it, but then put your dog in a time-out spot. This is different from his crate or his "special place" because those are areas where he is rewarded. A time-out spot is not a reward location; it is someplace where you know he is safe, but you can leave him and walk away. A pen or small bathroom (with no chewable items in it) works well. Make sure that you give him this time-out immediately after he nips so that it is crystal clear which behavior is undesirable. Don't leave him there for long or he will forget why he is there; he shouldn't be confined for more than a minute. What you want is a quick, short, and dramatic response to a behavior that you will not tolerate. This may take a few repetitions, but again, Rat Terriers are smart and your buddy will figure out that a nip means no more interaction with you. This removal from your presence is a big punishment for a Rat Terrier because his main goal is to be with you.

and on the fact that whatever game you were playing with him ended abruptly. Nipping can lead to biting, and that is not acceptable behavior in any dog.

Chapter
8

Activities With
Your Rat Terrier

Have ever watched one of those sports movies glorifying how teammates bond as they practice together? You may laugh, but that experience is not so different from doing activities with your Rat Terrier. You will learn to read each other's signals and body language. You become comrades, and you will learn to appreciate how hard your dog tries to "get it right" in order to please you. If the activity includes exercise for one or both of you, so much the better. A well-exercised dog is a happy dog and one who is less apt to have problem behaviors.

Traveling With Your Rat Terrier

One of the great things about your Rat Terrier is his size. He is a pick-up-and-go dog—easy to take with you when you travel. Therefore, you need to know how to take him along so that you both enjoy the trip. The key is to research and plan the trip in advance.

First, check that your pet is up to date with all of his vaccinations. Get your veterinarian to print out a copy of his medical records for you, and make a couple of copies to take along with you. Airlines will require a signed health

Make sure that your dog is safely secured if you are traveling by car.

RAT TERRIERS AND AGILITY

"Rat Terriers are naturals for agility—quick, intelligent, and willing to please. The outstanding agility prospects really stand out in their litter—these are the ones who are confident in new situations, enjoy exploring, yet come running when called!"

—Valerie Luchsinger, Ratitatt Rat Terriers

certificate from your veterinarian.

It is also important to make sure that your dog has clear identification on him. He needs to have a collar with a phone number and/or e-mail address on it. In addition, it's a good idea to have an identification microchip inserted by your veterinarian before you leave home. This is one of those cases where "an ounce of prevention is worth a pound of cure."

By Car

Most trips are going to be by automobile, so give your dog a chance to go on short rides to get over any car anxieties. Often, a dog's only car ride is to the veterinarian. If he doesn't like going there—and lots of dogs don't—he may have fear associated with car travel. So start taking him on short rides to fun-filled destinations such as a dog park, a favorite friend's house, or even a dog-friendly pet shop. Some dogs do better in a crate if they are used to one. My dogs race to get into crates in the back of the car and are nervous when they are loose. Always restrain your dog in a car

seat if he is not in a crate—in an accident, your dog could becomes a projectile. Restraining him is a safety measure, not a punishment.

If your dog really hates car rides, talk to your veterinarian. Anti-anxiety medications are available, but I strongly recommend using positive reinforcement training before dispensing any medications to your Rat Terrier.

Once your dog has accepted the car, plan your trip to accommodate his needs, as well as yours. Your adult Rat Terrier will need a regular rest stop every four to five hours to relieve himself. Breaks for puppies need to be more often and are determined by age. A break should give your dog time to exercise, relieve himself, and drink. Remember, some exercise along the way is important for you and your dog. It relieves a lot of his anxiety to spend some quality time with you, and it will tire him out. If he is tired, he will sleep better during the trip and will not keep you up at night once you get to your destination. I try not to feed my dogs

Traveling with your dog is a great bonding opportunity.

while they are on a car trip, but this only works for short trips. If you are on the road for a long trip, you may want to look up the names of some veterinary clinics or hospitals along the way and jot down their location and phone numbers. This little precaution lessens my anxiety about long car trips.

By Air

Air travel is not designed for dogs, and some airlines refuse to carry pets, so check ahead about your particular carrier. However, if your dog is a small Rat Terrier who can stand up comfortably in a crate that is not higher than 9 to 10 inches (23 to 25.4 cm) and 22 inches long (56 cm), many airlines will permit him to travel inside the airline cabin with you. The size limitation is because his crate must be able to fit in the space below the seat in front of you. Although your dog may be on board with you, airlines prohibit taking him out of the crate, so he needs to be able to stay in his crate happily.

Any crate larger than 9 to 10 inches (23 to 25.4 cm) high must go into the cargo hold. All airlines charge fees for pets, whether they travel in the cabin or in the cargo area. My daughter's dog has traveled often, and he is too large for the cabin. On the other hand, I avoid flying with my dogs whenever possible. If you must fly with your Rat Terrier, call ahead for requirements and restriction information. Your dog will have to be in an acceptable crate, and you must present required documents and identification. Many airlines refuse to accept dogs in the cargo area if either the departure or arrival city has a temperature (or is forecasted to have) of either below 20°F (-6.5°C) or above 95°F (35°C). The rules are even more stringent for short-nosed dogs, such as Pugs.

Airlines are also selective about the kinds of crates they accept, so be sure to check that yours is adequate. You don't want to arrive at the airport to find that your dog cannot go with you after all. Approved pet carriers are made of

Puppy Love

PUPPIES AND TRAVEL

Not all trips are appropriate for dogs—especially puppies. If you can't or don't want to take your puppy with you on a trip, see if you can have a friend or pet-sitting service stay with him. Interview your prospective dog sitter in your house to see how she and your pet get along. If you are using a professional pet-sitting service, it is not a bad idea to pay for a few visits before you actually need them. That will give all of the involved parties a chance to see how the upcoming trip may work out.

Consider some of the following items when preparing for your separation:

- describe what the pet sitter might expect from your pet—favorite places to sleep, to eat, to hide

- describe any unusual habit (for example, don't be alarmed if my puppy often barks in his sleep)

- make it clear what areas are off-limits for your pet (perhaps the laundry room because cleanser is stored where puppy can find it); don't expect your pup to tell the sitter about these spots!

hard plastic with holes for ventilation. At least 33 percent of the openings must be located in the top half of the carrier, and the carrier must have rims to prevent ventilation openings from being blocked by other cargo. Wire crates are not permitted, and soft-sided crates are only allowed in the cabin. The crate must be big enough to allow the animal to stand, turn around, and lie down in comfortably. It must have a leak-proof floor, covered with a towel or other absorbent lining.

Crates and carriers must have handles so that airline employees don't have to put their fingers inside the container. The crate must also contain a water and food dish, along with feeding instructions and a signed document stating that your pet was offered food and water within four hours of your scheduled departure. Mark the crate with your pet's name and your contact information. Write "Live Animal" on the top and side of the carrier. If you are changing airlines during the course

Today, more and more people are vacationing with their pets.

of the trip, don't forget to check with each airline about its rules.

Recently, some pet-friendly airways have been established to cater exclusively to pets. These flights have no human passengers on board other than the airline's pet tenders. These flights are not as expensive as you might guess. They are worth looking into, but their routes and schedules are limited.

Lodging

If your destination involves staying at a hotel, motel, or bed and breakfast, make sure that you and your pet will be welcome. More and more hotels are becoming pet friendly, but some advertise that they are and simply provide a kennel on their grounds. What you and your Rat Terrier are looking for is lodging that allows your pet to stay in your room. Some places offer amenities such as dog beds, special meals, and even dog spas and day care. Remember, none of these extras come free, so be sure to inquire about costs. Many establishments charge a nonrefundable pet deposit, a daily fee, and sometimes an additional cleaning fee. Many websites and magazines are available to help you sort through the dog-friendly places out there.

A final word of warning: If you are traveling with your pet and have found suitable travel and overnight

SPORTS AND SPORTS INJURIES

Before participating in any sport, have your veterinarian examine your pet first. Rat Terriers who have a medical history or joint-related problems should not participate in any agility training for example. Too much and too sudden exercise isn't advised for overweight dogs, either; they should diet first and train later. All dogs should be treated as well as human athletes and be given time to warm up.

Running and jumping on hard surfaces can be hard on paws and joints. Train on carpeted or grassy surfaces instead of concrete. Keep jumps at the appropriate height—usually shoulder height—and trim your dog's nails regularly so that he will not hurt himself upon landing. Finally, never push your dog too hard, and keep training sessions short. Fatigue is a leading cause of sports injuries for dogs and people.

accommodations, you still need to make sure that any tourist spots you want to visit permit pets. A dog can die if he is left in a hot car while his owner is visiting a site that does not permit pets inside. In these cases, it's preferable to leave him in the hotel while you sightsee. This is another good reason to take a crate along on your trip: It is much safer to leave your Rat Terrier in his crate for an hour or two while you are out than to have the hotel or motel cleaning person open the door and let your dog escape.

Sports

If you want to spend quality time with your dog and meet some nice four-footed and two-footed friends, you might be ready to take up a dog sport or activity. There are many to choose from for all sorts of canine and human temperaments and abilities. Usually, Rat Terriers are up for anything, so you might want to try several.

Agility

Agility—which consists of a timed obstacle course—is the fastest-growing

Agility is the fastest-growing sport in the world of dogs.

sport in the world of dogs, and Rat Terriers are savvy competitors. Border Collies, Shetland Sheepdogs, and Australian Shepherds may dominate the sport for speed, but most Rat Terriers are excellent at navigating through a course of jumps, tunnels, A-frames, rings, seesaws, and weave poles. What more could an energetic dog ask for? If you and your Rat Terrier seek this route of competition, your dog can move up through the three levels of degrees.

Conformation (Dog Shows)

In addition to all of the other activities mentioned in this chapter, you and your Rat Terrier might want to know how he stacks up against the competition in the conformation ring. Your timing could not be better because the American Kennel Club (AKC) opened its Miscellaneous Class to Rat Terriers June 30, 2010. Normally, it takes a minimum of 18 months after that for a breed to achieve full status so that dogs can compete in regular breed classes. In the miscellaneous and regular classes, conformation is determined by how closely your dog conforms to the breed standard, which is discussed in Chapter 2 of this book. The standard describes the dog's looks, movement, and temperament. The evaluator, or dog show judge in this case, will attempt to select the dog who most closely conforms

to the breed standard. To compete in conformation classes, your Rat Terrier cannot be neutered or spayed because the original idea of a dog show was to select the best dogs for breeding. Therefore, you will want to determine when your dog is quite young if you wish to show him. Visit some dog shows and meet people who show Rat Terriers. If you strike up a relationship with some, you might want them to look at your puppy and give their opinion as to the viability of

Conformation evaluates a dog against the breed standard.

showing your dog. Showing a dog can become a full-time occupation. Many people breed dogs solely for the chance to win in conformation shows, but never succeed at the highest levels. With so many unwanted dogs and puppies in shelters, it may not be the best decision to keep an unneutered dog or unspayed bitch unless you decide to commit to the world of showing your dog in conformation.

Once the Rat Terrier breed receives its approval to be a fully recognized AKC breed, you will be able to show your dog in regular conformation classes at AKC dog shows. Showing a dog successfully in conformation looks easier than it is. For example, to win a coveted AKC dog show such as the Westminster Kennel Club show, a dog has to have previously received his championship at several other shows. If a dog has acquired enough show points along the way (points accrue according to the number of dogs the winner defeats in each class), he might be eligible to compete at Westminster. Once entered, a dog must win his breed class by being picked as the best Rat Terrier. Then he must compete against all of the terriers who were judged to be best of their terrier breeds. The winner of the Terrier Group goes in the ring against the winners of each of the other six Group winners: Sporting,

An experienced conformation participant can tell you if your dog is a good show prospect.

Hound, Working, Herding, Toy, and Non-Sporting. The final judge determines which one of these group winners adheres closest to the standard for that breed of dog—and that dog is selected to receive the title Best in Show.

Earthdog

As terriers, Rat Terriers are eligible to compete in earthdog trials. These trials simulate the work of terriers in pursuit of vermin. Earthdog trials use wooden tunnels that are dug into the ground, with a cage at the end containing prey (usually a rat). When the terrier is given the command, he scoots through the tunnel and "works" the prey. Working is defined as barking, digging, scratching, or biting the bars of the cage. The dog receives points for speed in the tunnel and the amount of time he works. Junior Earthdog (JE), Senior Earthdog (SE), and Master Earthdog (ME) titles are awarded to dogs as they pass tests of increasing difficulty.

Rally

Rally is a relatively new dog sport, one that is growing in popularity because it is enjoyable for both dog handler and dog. In rally, the handler and dog are a team, passing along a prescribed path

Because terriers like to dig to find vermin, earthdog may be the perfect sport for your dog.

and performing tasks at each marked locations. The rally judge tells the team to begin, and the handler and dog move forward through 10 to 20 stations. The number of stations is determined by the level of competition. Each location or station has a sign on it instructing the handler what task is to be performed. Typical signs tell the team to go fast or slow, to halt with the dog sitting in a *heel* position, to turn left or right, to circle, reverse direction, do a *sit-stay-recall*, or perform other basic obedience exercises.

One feature of rally that appeals to many dog people is that the handler may openly communicate with her dog throughout the event. She can praise, encourage, clap her hands, slap her leg encouragingly, and even use multiple commands for her dog. The only limitation is that the handler cannot touch her dog or use any sort of intimidating sounds or motions.

Judging in rally is not as rigorous as in traditional obedience classes. The objective of the sport is to encourage dogs to behave well in the home, in public

Rat Terriers are adept at a variety of dog sports.

Check It Out

TRAVEL CHECKLIST

- ✓ bags to pick up waste
- ✓ blanket and/or dog bed
- ✓ dog seat belt or crate / kennel
- ✓ health certificate (obtain from your vet)
- ✓ leash
- ✓ lists of rest stops and veterinary hospitals

- ✓ medications, if applicable
- ✓ one or two toys
- ✓ treats
- ✓ water and bowls
- ✓ your dog's medical records (including vaccine history)

places, and in the presence of other dogs. Several levels of competition exist; in AKC rally, the Novice level consists of 10 to 15 stations, and the course is completed on leash. The Advanced level is more difficult, with 12 to 17 stations, with the dog off-leash. The third and last level is Excellent, and the team must negotiate 15 to 20 stations with the dog off-leash and with only verbal praises permitted.

Therapy Work

If you decide that your Rat Terrier is more than a pretty face, and you have time on your hands (and his paws), you might consider sharing your dog's company with others. A well-trained dog is often welcomed as a visitor to hospitals, nursing homes, and other places that have pet therapy programs. Contact these places first, to see what their requirements are for visiting therapy pets. The minimum is usually the Canine Good Citizen certificate, but many organizations ask that their therapy dogs have higher degrees or pass additional tests.

Assistance Dogs

The trained Rat Terrier can become a wonderful assistance or service dog. Rat Terriers are clever dogs, able to understand the many tasks and clues necessary to aid someone who needs help. They are a perfect size to fetch and retrieve items. They are smart and agile enough to learn how to speed-dial emergency numbers and even unscrew bottle caps!

Chapter
9

Health of Your
Rat Terrier

When you invite a Rat Terrier into your family, you are accepting him "in sickness and in health." Because your dog cannot verbally tell you when something hurts, it will be your responsibility to pay close attention to his body language to monitor his health. Your job can be made easier if you are aware of some common symptoms of illnesses and available remedies for your pup.

After you and your family, his vet is your Rat Terrier's most important person.

Finding the Right Vet

Coming after you and your family, his veterinarian is your Rat Terrier's most important person. So if you don't already have a veterinarian, how do you find one? Do some research. Start thinking about finding a vet before acquiring a new pet or before you move to a new area. If you are moving and already have a veterinarian for your Rat Terrier, ask your current veterinarian for recommendations. But if you don't have that source, ask friends, co-workers, or other pet owners in your area for recommendations. Finally, try the Internet and the Yellow Pages, both of which list veterinarians.

If you are moving or getting a new dog, it's a good idea to have a veterinarian in place before you actually need one. Schedule a visit with a prospective vet as soon as you arrive in your new neighborhood or before acquiring your new dog. Your newly found veterinarian can suggest ways to help your Rat Terrier adjust to his home and educate you about any local health risks to your pet, especially when new geographical areas have unfamiliar, harmful plants or pests. Some veterinarians charge for this type of consultation, but others do not. Ask first.

Evaluate the Services

Once you have located a possible veterinarian, evaluate the services her office offers. Some things are apparent

Puppy Love

SCHEDULE OF PUPPY VACCINATIONS Per the American Veterinary Medical Association (AVMA)	
Age	**Vaccine**
5 weeks	Parvovirus for puppies at high risk due to possible exposure
6 to 9 weeks	Combination vaccine without leptospirosis, with coronavirus where this is a concern
12 weeks and older	Rabies (local laws may dictate the schedule)
12 to 16 weeks	Combination vaccine; leptospirosis and/or Lyme when puppy lives in or is traveling to an area where either of these occurs
Adult boosters	Combination vaccine; leptospirosis and/or Lyme when dog lives in or is traveling to an area where either of these occurs

right away. The reception area should be clean and pet friendly—not crowded so that waiting pets are too close to each other. You don't want your dog all bunched up with other pets—some of those pets are sick, after all.

The staff should be helpful and knowledgeable. Find out what hours the office is open and if these fit with your schedule. Does the office handle its own X-rays, ultrasound, blood work, EKG, endoscopy, or other diagnostic tests? If not, where will you go if any of these

procedures are necessary? Inquire what happens if your pet needs emergency attention after hours. Find out about the staff. Who will be taking care of your dog while he is in the office or if he has to stay for a procedure? Will your dog be treated only by the veterinarian or by technicians and assistants? Query each one of them about their individual training and their experience. If your veterinarian is a specialist, inquire about board certification. To be board certified, the veterinarian has studied an additional two to four years in her specialty area and has passed a rigorous exam.

Ask if the veterinarian has other Rat Terriers as patients. These dogs are rare in many parts of the United States, so don't be put off by a veterinarian who has no experience with Rat Terriers. Most veterinarians are able to use the Internet to research and communicate with other veterinarians to aid in diagnosis; therefore, it is reasonable to ask if this veterinarian is Internet savvy.

Ask About Fees

Before you leave, ask about the fees associated with regular procedures such as checkups, spaying, neutering, etc. This will give you some idea as to the annual costs you will be paying.

The First Vet Visit

If your new Rat Terrier is a puppy, take him to the veterinarian within the first couple of days after you get him—sooner if there are any signs of illness. A new puppy from a reputable breeder should come with all of his medical records and a health guarantee stating that if the puppy has a severe health problem you can return him. The veterinarian will perform a physical check of your puppy. She will look at the puppy's eyes, listen to his heart and lungs, and inspect his nose for discharge to rule out any respiratory infection. The puppy's throat and tonsils will all be examined, and his mouth will be checked for bad breath and pale gums. The veterinarian will insert an otoscope into the pup's ear. This tool magnifies the dog's ear canal and eardrum so that the veterinarian can see mites or infections.

The Annual Vet Visit

The annual visit for your adult Rat Terrier is not very different from the one he received as a puppy—except that the

On a personal level, I interviewed two veterinarians when I moved to my current home. Both had been recommended by my dog's breeder, and from a first impression, I found them to be about equal. I ended up selecting the one closer to my residence. I decided that it was a convenience for me and that, in an emergency, closer could be important. This choice has paid additional dividends over the years, because my nearby veterinarian was able to stop by my house when it was necessary to euthanize two of my pets on different occasions. Once, he showed up on the Fourth of July when a dog suffering from cancer needed immediate attention. I think I made a good choice.

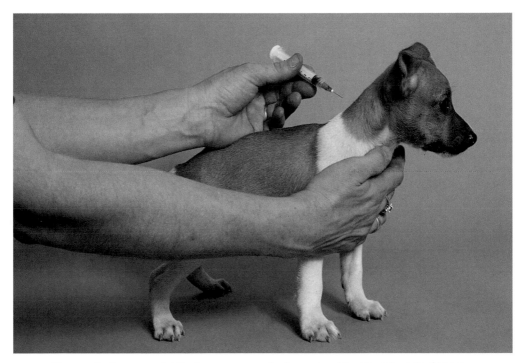

The vaccinations your Rat Terrier puppy needs depend on his age and medical history.

vaccinations are fewer. To assist your veterinarian and technicians do their jobs as best they can, train your dog to behave well during vet visits. He needs to tolerate being handled by strangers. When you groom him, mimic the motions that he will have to endure during his checkup: Stand him on a table, have him lie down, roll him on his sides, open his mouth, look in his ears, check his coat, handle his paws, and manipulate his feet. Reward him for his good behavior with some treats.

Vaccinations

The vaccinations your Rat Terrier puppy needs depend on his age and his medical history. The American Veterinary Medical Association (AVMA) publishes a detailed list of vaccinations appropriate for puppies at different ages. At his first vet visit, the most common vaccination for your puppy is the DHPP, which combines canine distemper, canine hepatitis virus, parainfluenza, and parvovirus. Your veterinarian may wish to add an "L" to

Ask the Expert

The American Veterinary Medical Association (AVMA) suggests that your dog should visit a veterinarian once a year. During this annual visit, your vet will use a stethoscope to listen to your dog's heart and lungs, examine the dog's overall body health, perform fecal and blood checks to diagnose parasites, and administer medications and vaccinations when necessary. The annual visit may not seem important, but it is. Your veterinarian can often hear heart abnormalities and notice the earliest symptoms of diseases, such as cancer. Early detection of many ailments can be key to restoring your dog to health and ensuring him of a long life.

those letters if she thinks that your pup should be vaccinated for leptospirosis. This decision is usually determined by where you live and the strains of the disease in your area.

Most puppies and dogs don't mind their vaccinations at all, but if you feel guilty when your Rat Terrier turns those liquid eyes on you, here is an alphabetical list of the common diseases that your dog will be vaccinated against. Better sad puppy eyes than any preventable disease. Consult with your veterinarian about which shots are necessary for your dog and which ones are not.

Bordetella
Bordetella, also known as kennel cough, is a contagious upper respiratory ailment. The symptoms are similar to those of parainfluenza—a harsh, dry cough aggravated by activity or excitement. Coughing may be followed by gagging or retching in an attempt to bring up small amounts of mucus clogging the dog's throat. If your dog is coughing, take him to the veterinarian for treatment to prevent secondary infections.

Coronavirus
Coronavirus is highly contagious; it is somewhat similar to parvovirus in its symptoms, producing diarrhea that often contains blood. A dog may be less likely to vomit with coronavirus than with parvovirus. Both diseases are often fatal, and your dog will need professional attention. There is a vaccine to prevent coronavirus, but ask your veterinarian if it is necessary or not. Many veterinarians feel that this is an optional vaccination in areas where the disease is not prevalent.

Distemper
Distemper is a contagious, incurable, often fatal, multi-systemic viral disease.

It affects the respiratory, gastrointestinal, and central nervous systems. It used to be a leading killer in puppies, but the vaccine has been highly successful in limiting outbreaks.

Hepatitis

Infectious canine hepatitis (ICH) is a highly contagious viral disease, but it is not related to human hepatitis. ICH primarily affects the dog's liver, but it can spread to other organs. Symptoms range in severity and include loss of appetite, nausea, vomiting, light-colored stool, and stomach enlargement, tonsillitis, pale gums, and jaundice (yellowing of the whites of the dog's eyes). The disease is treated with antibiotics, a low-protein diet, and occasionally with immunosuppressants (medications to inhibit the immune system), but the prognosis is often determined by the extent of liver damage.

Leptospirosis

Lepto is caused by the *Leptospira* bacteria, which are present in the urine of infected animals or in drinking water or food that has been contaminated by the bacteria. Dogs who are infected with lepto show signs of fever, muscle weakness, vomiting, lethargy, abdominal pain, and kidney or liver failure. A dog with any of these symptoms must be seen by a veterinarian. Your dog's lifestyle and geographical area will determine if he needs this vaccination, so check with your veterinarian for advice.

Lyme Disease

Canine Lyme disease is caused by a bacteria transmitted by deer tick bites if the tick remains on the dog's skin for 24 to 48 hours. Early symptoms in dogs are fever, loss of appetite, swollen lymph nodes, inflamed joints, and limping. Later

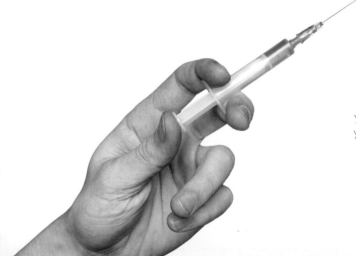

Your veterinarian will advise you on which vaccines your Rat Terrier needs.

symptoms include lethargy, lack of body coordination, and neurological problems. If the disease is not treated, it can permanently damage the nerves, joints, heart, and kidney. Treatment includes the use of antibiotics for three to four weeks. There is a vaccine for Lyme disease, so check with your veterinarian to see if you live in a geographical area where deer ticks—and therefore the disease—are common. Also, be sure to tell your veterinarian if you and your Rat Terrier have travel plans that will take you into an area where Lyme disease is prevalent.

Parainfluenza

This is a common cause of a canine upper respiratory disease complex, often called kennel cough. Symptoms are coughing that may become more severe if the dog is active or excited. The disease usually runs its course in five to ten days, but it may lead to secondary bacterial infections, so you need to have any coughing dog seen by your veterinarian, who will usually suggest a cough medication and prescribe antibiotics.

Parvovirus

This is a highly contagious canine virus. Symptoms of intestinal parvo include vomiting and bloody diarrhea, and the disease may develop into cardiac and respiratory problems. The virus is spread by contaminated feces, and it can remain in the soil for several months. Parvo is often fatal in puppies. The best prevention is vaccination, but there is some new evidence that the virus may be mutating into several strains. If you notice any parvo-like symptoms in your Rat Terrier (especially a puppy), take him to your veterinarian as soon as possible. Treatment includes intravenous fluids and antibiotics. In severe cases, a dog may need anti-vomiting drugs, corticosteroids, and even blood transfusions.

Rabies

Rabies is a deadly virus that attacks the nervous system and causes a type of encephalitis. Rabies is carried in the saliva of an infected animal. If your dog has been bitten by an animal who might be rabid, take him to the veterinarian immediately. Do not wait for symptoms such as behavioral changes, fever, slow eye reflexes, and chewing at the bite site to develop. Once the symptoms are evident, it is almost always too late to treat the animal. The best prevention is to regularly vaccinate your dog for rabies according on the schedule required by your local laws and to avoid animals who live in the wild.

Parasites

Your vet will check your Rat Terrier for parasites. From time to time, some of them occur in the best of doggy households, so you need to learn how to recognize and eliminate them.

Internal Parasites

Even a healthy-looking dog can have hidden internal parasites, such as worms. Puppies are especially susceptible hosts to these unwanted visitors. Early detection is important, so it is advisable that you take a stool sample to your veterinarian when your dog has his checkup even if you do not suspect a problem. There are remedies available to eliminate worms, but the medication must target the precise type of worm your dog has. Therefore, you will need your veterinarian's insight when selecting the correct treatment for your dog.

Heartworms

Heartworms are transmitted from animal to animal by mosquito bites. The mosquito carries microfilariae, which in the dog's bloodstream, change into larvae and then into adult heartworms that invade the dog's lungs and blood vessels, leading to heart disease. The process from bite to heartworm takes about six months, so your veterinarian will regularly do a blood test for signs of heartworm once your dog is over the age of six months. The good news is that heartworm can be treated. (My bouncy little rescue dog can testify to that.) The better news is that heartworm infection is almost 100 percent preventable. Your veterinarian can prescribe an FDA-approved heartworm preventive that will work well for your Rat Terrier.

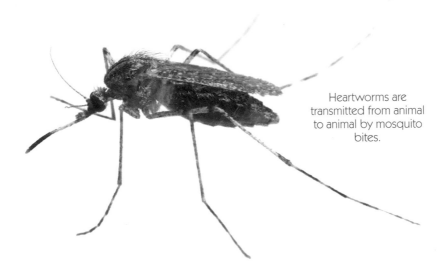

Heartworms are transmitted from animal to animal by mosquito bites.

SPAYING AND NEUTERING

The first visit to a veterinarian is a good time to discuss spaying or neutering your Rat Terrier. Unless you are absolutely committed to breeding your Rat Terrier, please spay females and neuter males. The simple surgery solves many problem behaviors and contributes to the health of your dog as he or she ages. I have no idea who started the age-old myth that a female dog needs to have one litter to develop a better temperament, but whoever it was needs to tour some of our overly packed animals shelters and see the number of old female dogs with illnesses that could have been prevented by spaying. The same must be said for male dogs. A neutered male dog is less prone to certain diseases and will be a delightful pet.

Hookworms

A hookworm latches onto your dog's intestinal lining with its hook-shaped teeth. Hookworms live in the soil, where they are accidentally ingested, or they can burrow into the dog through his skin. Symptoms include lethargy, diarrhea, and anemia. By examining your dog's feces, a veterinarian will be able to make a diagnosis and prescribe oral medication and preventive treatment.

Roundworms

Roundworms are a common parasite in the canine digestive tract—especially in puppies. A potbelly can be a symptom of infestation, but so can excessive thinness. The pup may have loose stools and/or vomiting, and the infection can spread to the lungs and cause pneumonia. Your veterinarian will examine a sample of your dog's feces to make the diagnosis and recommend treatment, which may involve repeated doses of dewormer spread over several weeks. Roundworms are less of a problem today because several heartworm preventives also kill roundworms.

Whipworms

Whipworms reside in your dog's intestine and can be detected by a veterinary examination of the feces. Although symptoms are rare at the beginning of an infection, the dog will eventually develop diarrhea. Standard heartworm medications contain preventives that are effective against whipworms as well.

External Parasites

External parasites, such as fleas and ticks, can be harmful to your dog. Not only do they live on his body, and in extreme cases, cause fatal anemia, they are also intermediate hosts that can spread tapeworms (which show up as tiny pieces of "rice" in your dog's stools) and Lyme disease to your pet.

Fleas

If your Rat Terrier is scratching a lot, check for fleas. Use a flea comb during your regular grooming, and you might catch one in the comb's narrow teeth.

More likely, you will see flea dirt, which looks like little dots of ground pepper. Drop one of those dots on a wet paper towel, and if it turns red, you are dealing with flea dirt. Fleas can make your dog miserable, cause skin reactions, and carry tapeworms, so take action. Fleas are difficult, but not impossible, to eliminate. Your veterinarian will be able to recommend medications for your dog and strategies to rid fleas from your dog's environment. Because some Rat Terriers

Check your dog for fleas and ticks after he's been playing outside.

are prone to allergies, you will have to be careful in selecting what you use. Don't overreact and start spraying, bombing, and dipping without research.

Ticks

Ticks are nasty parasites that can carry diseases. Before they feed, they look like tiny spiders (they are related), but when they have attached themselves to your dog, they swell up and resemble small beans. If ticks are a problem in your area, look for them during your grooming sessions and ask your veterinarian for preventive medication. Again, be careful not to use any substances that could set off an allergic reaction.

If you find a tick on your dog, you will want to remove it promptly. This is easy when the tick is moving and has not yet "latched on" to the dog, but don't use your bare hands. Pick up the loose tick with tweezers or by wrapping it in a tissue. Dispose of this unpleasant arachnid by

If ticks are a problem in your area, look for them during your grooming sessions.

YOUR DOG'S FIRST-AID KIT

Every dog owner should have a first-aid kit on hand for emergencies. Gather what you need before you need an item. No one wants to be running around looking for something in an emergency. (If you remove something from the kit, be sure to replace it!) Your first-aid kit should include:

- **Adhesive tape:** to secure bandages

- **Antibiotic cream:** for external wounds

- **Anti-diarrheal medication:** to treat diarrhea

- **Bandages:** several types to dress wounds or secure splints

- **Cold/heat packs (wrapped in a towel before applying):** to reduce swelling or warm a cold dog

- **Cotton balls:** for cleaning wounds

- **Digital rectal thermometer:** to check your pet's temperature rectally

- **Emergency information attached to container:** phone number of your veterinarian; copy of your dog's medical record, including vaccination record; and phone numbers for the local emergency veterinarian clinic, Animal Poison Control Center, and friend/relative/alternative dog caretaker

- **Eye dropper or syringe without needle:** to administer oral treatment or flush wounds

- **Gauze:** for wrapping wound or muzzling an injured animal

- **Hydrogen peroxide (3%):** to induce vomiting—but only if your veterinarian or the poison control center tells you to use it—and to clean wounds

- **Laxative:** to relieve constipation

- **Leash:** to transport your dog if he is mobile

- **Milk of magnesia and activated charcoal:** to absorb poison, but only if your veterinarian or the poison control center tells you to use it

- **Muzzle:** to secure your dog's mouth if he is in pain; do not use this if your dog is vomiting

- **Nonstick bandages, towels, strips of clean cloth:** to control bleeding and protect wounds

- **Petroleum Jelly:** to lubricate the thermometer

- **Scissors:** to cut bandages

- **Stretcher (large towel, blanket, bath mat):** to transport an immobile dog, you might want to use a board or even a door to stabilize him if you are unsure of internal injuries

- **Tweezers:** to remove foreign bodies

dropping it in a small container of rubbing alcohol. (I keep a small container at the ready.) The tick will die quickly and you can flush the jar contents down the toilet.

If you find a tick that has latched on to the dog, you will need to address the problem differently. There are theories about forcing it to release by coating it with petroleum jelly or putting rubbing alcohol on it. I am told that his works eventually, but I want that little monster off my pet now! The longer a tick is on the dog, the more chance there is of disease spreading into the dog's bloodstream. I take my fine-tipped tweezers and pinch down as near to the tick's head as possible. Then I pluck the tick off and dispose of it in rubbing alcohol, as just described. Avoid handling the tick, and be sure to wash your hands thoroughly after dealing with one.

Breed-Specific Illnesses

Rat Terriers are generally healthy dogs, but you should be aware of some issues that occur in the breed—and in other breeds as well.

Allergies

Rat Terriers are not the only dogs to suffer from allergies, but their owners need to be aware that the breed seems to have a tendency to develop them. Allergies are categorized into three types.

A *contact allergy* is a reaction to a foreign substance—it's what happens when a person who is allergic to poison ivy comes in contact with the plant. Rat Terriers have can have allergic reactions to chemicals such as powders, shampoos, insect bites, and even fabrics such as the filling in his dog bed.

A *food allergy* is caused by a reaction to ingredients in your dog's meals or treats. This is one reason why it is important to monitor your dog if you are making changes in his diet. Some owners think that corn can be a common culprit, but others disagree.

An *inhalant allergy* is caused when your dog breathes in airborne particles such as dust, pollen, and mildew.

Treating allergies requires a fair amount of sleuthing. Take your dog to his veterinarian for medication that may help relieve his symptoms and to review possible causes. You will have to eliminate as many sources as possible, both dietary and environmental.

Cancer

Cancer is the leading cause of death for all dogs. Constant medical advancements are being made in the treatment of differing cancers, but early detection is key. Know the common manifestations of canine cancer, and check your dog regularly for any warning signs. According to the AVMA, the ten most common signs of cancer are:

- abnormal swellings that persist or continue to grow
- sores that do not heal
- weight loss
- loss of appetite
- bleeding or discharge from any body opening
- offensive odor
- difficulty eating or swallowing
- hesitation to exercise or loss of stamina
- persistent lameness or stiffness
- difficulty breathing, urinating, or defecating

Veterinary oncologists specialize in treating dogs with cancer. Treatments are as varied as the disease, which can attack in many forms, but the current therapies often include chemotherapy, radiation therapy, and the surgical removal of tumors.

Congestive Heart Failure

Congestive heart failure affects all dogs, but it is especially common in the smaller breeds. You should know the symptoms: decreasing energy, difficult breathing, and coughing. Congestive heart failure cannot be remedied, but you and your veterinarian can often manage it with medications and a special diet.

Demodectic Mange

People don't seem to agree on the title for this ailment, but they do know it is caused by the demodex mite, which lives in a dog's hair follicle. This is perfectly normal, harmless to humans, and a balanced part of the canine environment. Sometimes a puppy will develop a skin rash during stressful times, such as when teething, but that is usually not a cause for concern. However, when an adult Rat Terrier continues to exhibit patches of red, scaly, balding skin, you need to take your dog to the veterinarian to prevent the rash from spreading. Research indicates a genetic link to this problem. The theory is that infected dogs have inherited an

A scissors bite is preferred by the breed standard.

CHECKLIST FOR A HEALTHY RAT TERRIER

✓ Find a good veterinarian for your dog.

✓ Take your dog for an annual checkup.

✓ Keep your dog's

✓ vaccinations current.

✓ Examine your dog regularly.

✓ Keep emergency phone numbers and a first-aid kit on hand.

autoimmune defect that allows the mite to multiply at a faster than usual rate. Dogs who suffer from demodectic mange should not be included in a responsible Rat Terrier breeding program. Most demodectic mange is treated topically with lotions, dips, and shampoos, but some persistent cases may require antibiotics.

Hip and/or Knee Dysplasia

Hip or knee dysplasia is caused by an abnormal joint structure and associated connective tissues (muscles and ligaments). The malformation can cause pain and lameness and may increase with age. The ailment is thought to be genetic but may also have a connection to those dog breeds whose puppies tend to grow at a fast rate. It is also linked to obesity in puppies and dogs. Your veterinarian will use radiology to diagnose the disease and advise you on treatment. Surgery is sometimes an option.

Incorrect Bite or Malocclusion

The Rat Terrier breed standard states that a scissors bite is preferred, and a level bite is acceptable. Three types of misaligned jaws result in incorrect bites. If the upper jaw extends out farther than the lower jaw, the bite is called overshot. When the lower jaw juts out, it is called an undershot bite. This type of jaw is acceptable in some dog breeds, such as the Bulldog. The third undesirable jaw formation is called a wry mouth and occurs when the left and right sides of the jaw do not grow evenly and the jaw actually twists slightly. These bite problems can correct as a young puppy grows to about ten months of age. After that time, it is unlikely that the jaw will straighten enough to meet the standard. If the problem is so severe that the Rat Terrier has difficulty eating or chewing, he might need corrective surgery. This can involve the filing and/or removal of some teeth. In addition to jaw problems, Rat Terriers do have a propensity for crooked teeth and retained baby teeth, which are also considered faults and may need medical attention. Dental procedures, including tooth extractions, can reduce the problems. However, malocclusion is inherited, so dogs with the condition should not be included in a breeding program

Patellar Luxation or Slipped Stifles

This is not just a problem for Rat Terriers but for many small dog breeds. A dog's patella is similar to our kneecap. This canine kneecap is held in place by grooves in the thighbone or femur. When these grooves are too shallow, the patella can slip out of place, which is called luxation. This causes lameness and pain, which can increase to the point of crippling the dog. If the condition is severe, consult with your veterinarian about a surgical remedy.

Primary Lens Luxation (PLL)

PLL is an eye problem faced by many terrier breeds. The eye lens is held in place by ligaments, which are weakened in a dog with PLL, and this allows the lens to slip out of place. Lens luxation can lead to painful inflammation and pressure in the eye and often to blindness. If your dog's eyes are painful, teary, red, or cloudy, take him to see your veterinarian. Surgical removal of the lens and medications (both oral and topical) may relieve much of the pain associated with the condition. PLL is an inherited disorder, and there is a simple test to help you learn if your dog is at risk for it. The test kit is available for purchase through the Orthopedic Foundation for Animals (OFA) (www.ofa.org). Take a swab of your dog's mouth and mail it back to the OFA, which will tell you the result and add your dog to its database. When you purchase a Rat Terrier from a breeder, you should ask for the parents' tests results. Dogs with PLL should not be part of a breeding program.

Alternative Therapies

Recently, more and more dog owners are trying alternative medicine for their pets. Some of the most popular are *acupuncture* to assist in the control pain and cure chronic ailments using very fine needles applied to certain pressure points on the body; *chiropractic care* to provide spinal adjustments and relieve pain; *herbal treatments* to treat ailments using plants and extracts; *homeopathy* to relieve ailments by introducing tiny amounts of substances that will boost the dog's own immune system; *massage* to increase circulation and ease pain; and *nutritional supplements*. Increasing numbers of veterinarians are accepting the use of alternative medications, so it is worthwhile to discuss some of these

As your dog ages, his senses may dull, and he will slow down.

remedies with your vet if you choose to try them. Open discussion of alternative therapies is also important to prevent any possible adverse effects if your dog is taking traditional medications, or if you have a dog who is allergic to many substances. If your veterinarian is unable to suggest a source for alternative medicine, contact the American Holistic Veterinary Medical Association (AHVMA) (www.ahvma.org) for the names of practitioners in your area.

Senior Dogs

With good care, good genes, and good fortune, your Rat Terrier will live 12 to 18 healthy years. The American Animal Hospital Association (AAHA) calculates that old age spans the last quarter of a dog's life. Therefore, you might want to estimate that your dog's "golden years" begin somewhere between 10 and 12 years of age.

Some veterinarians like to see their senior dogs twice a year, to watch for any symptoms of ailments that might be helped by early diagnosis. They may want to do some laboratory tests to show your Rat Terrier's baseline values so that they will recognize even slightly abnormal results in the future. The AAHA recommends about 20 tests, including a blood count, urinalysis, fecal analysis, serum electrolytes, and eye and dental exams. The AVMA lists eight common

Obesity is common in older dogs, so pay close attention to your senior's nutritional needs.

ailments of old age: cancer, heart disease, kidney/urinary tract disease, liver disease, diabetes, joint or bone disease, senility, and weakness. You and your veterinarian should decide which are the most important tests for your dog based on his history.

As your dog ages, his senses may dull, and he will slow down. The AVMA says that you should expect certain behavior changes in an older dog: increased reaction to sounds, increased vocalization, confusion, disorientation, decreased interaction with humans, increased irritability, decreased response to commands, increased aggressive/ protective behavior, increased anxiety, house soiling, decreased self-hygiene, repetitive activity, increased wandering, and changes in sleep habits. With these in mind, try to keep your Rat Terrier active and engaged in age- and health-appropriate activities.

Obesity is common in older dogs, so pay close attention to your senior's nutritional needs and to the amount of activity he is getting. He may also develop ailments that are painful, so he may need pain management medication. You owe your Rat Terrier attention, kindness, and consideration as he maintains his dignity into old age.

Resources

Associations and Organizations

Breed Clubs

American Kennel Club (AKC)
5580 Centerview Drive
Raleigh, NC 27606
Telephone: (919) 233-9767
Fax: (919) 233-3627
E-Mail: info@akc.org
www.akc.org

Canadian Kennel Club (CKC)
89 Skyway Avenue, Suite 100
Etobicoke, Ontario M9W 6R4
Telephone: (416) 675-5511
Fax: (416) 675-6506
E-Mail: information@ckc.ca
www.ckc.ca

Federation Cynologique Internationale (FCI)
Secretariat General de la FCI
Place Albert 1er, 13
B – 6530 Thuin
Belqique
www.fci.be

Rat Terrier Club of America (RTCA)
47044 5th St. West
Lancaster, CA 93534-7501
Telephone: (661) 945-5663
www.ratterrierclub.com

The Kennel Club
1 Clarges Street
London
W1J 8AB
Telephone: 0870 606 6750
Fax: 0207 518 1058
www.the-kennel-club.org.uk

United Kennel Club (UKC)
100 E. Kilgore Road
Kalamazoo, MI 49002-5584
Telephone: (269) 343-9020
Fax: (269) 343-7037
E-Mail: pbickell@ukcdogs.com
www.ukcdogs.com

Pet Sitters

National Association of Professional Pet Sitters
15000 Commerce Parkway, Suite C
Mt. Laurel, New Jersey 08054
Telephone: (856) 439-0324
Fax: (856) 439-0525
E-Mail: napps@ahint.com
www.petsitters.org

Pet Sitters International
201 East King Street
King, NC 27021-9161
Telephone: (336) 983-9222
Fax: (336) 983-5266
E-Mail: info@petsit.com
www.petsit.com

Rescue Organizations and Animal Welfare Groups

American Humane Association (AHA)
63 Inverness Drive East
Englewood, CO 80112
Telephone: (303) 792-9900
Fax: 792-5333
www.americanhumane.org

American Society for the Prevention of Cruelty to Animals (ASPCA)
424 E. 92nd Street
New York, NY 10128-6804
Telephone: (212) 876-7700
www.aspca.org

The Humane Society of the United States (HSUS)
2100 L Street, NW
Washington DC 20037
Telephone: (202) 452-1100
www.hsus.org

Royal Society for the Prevention of Cruelty to
Animals (RSPCA)
RSPCA Enquiries Service
Wilberforce Way, Southwater,
Horsham, West Sussex RH13 9RS
United Kingdom
Telephone: 0870 3335 999
Fax: 0870 7530 284
www.rspca.org.uk

Sports
International Agility Link (IAL)
Global Administrator: Steve Drinkwater
E-Mail: yunde@powerup.au
www.agilityclick.com/~ial

The World Canine Freestyle Organization, Inc.
P.O. Box 350122
Brooklyn, NY 11235
Telephone: (718) 332-8336
Fax: (718) 646-2686
E-Mail: WCFODOGS@aol.com
www.worldcaninefreestyle.org

Therapy
Delta Society
875 124th Ave, NE, Suite 101
Bellevue, WA 98005
Telephone: (425) 679-5500
Fax: (425) 679-5539
E-Mail: info@DeltaSociety.org
www.deltasociety.org

Therapy Dogs Inc.
P.O. Box 20227
Cheyenne WY 82003
Telephone: (877) 843-7364
Fax: (307) 638-2079
E-Mail: therapydogsinc@qwestoffice.net
www.therapydogs.com

Therapy Dogs International (TDI)
88 Bartley Road
Flanders, NJ 07836
Telephone: (973) 252-9800
Fax: (973) 252-7171
E-Mail: tdi@gti.net
www.tdi-dog.org

Training
Association of Pet Dog Trainers (APDT)
150 Executive Center Drive Box 35
Greenville, SC 29615
Telephone: (800) PET-DOGS
Fax: (864) 331-0767
E-Mail: information@apdt.com
www.apdt.com

International Association of Animal Behavior
Consultants (IAABC)
565 Callery Road
Cranberry Township, PA 16066
E-Mail: info@iaabc.org
www.iaabc.org

National Association of Dog Obedience
Instructors (NADOI)
PMB 369
729 Grapevine Hwy.
Hurst, TX 76054-2085
www.nadoi.org

Veterinary and Health Resources
Academy of Veterinary Homeopathy (AVH)
P.O. Box 9280
Wilmington, DE 19809
Telephone: (866) 652-1590
Fax: (866) 652-1590
www.theavh.org

American Academy of Veterinary Acupuncture (AAVA)
P.O. Box 1058
Glastonbury, CT 06033
Telephone: (860) 632-9911
Fax: (860) 659-8772
www.aava.org

American Animal Hospital Association (AAHA)
12575 W. Bayaud Ave.
Lakewood, CO 80228
Telephone: (303) 986-2800
Fax: (303) 986-1700
E-Mail: info@aahanet.org
www.aahanet.org/index.cfm

American College of Veterinary Internal Medicine (ACVIM)
1997 Wadsworth Blvd., Suite A
Lakewood, CO 80214-5293
Telephone: (800) 245-9081
Fax: (303) 231-0880
Email: ACVIM@ACVIM.org
www.acvim.org

American College of Veterinary Ophthalmologists (ACVO)
P.O. Box 1311
Meridian, ID 83860
Telephone: (208) 466-7624
Fax: (208) 466-7693
E-Mail: office09@acvo.com
www.acvo.com

American Holistic Veterinary Medical Association (AHVMA)
2218 Old Emmorton Road
Bel Air, MD 21015
Telephone: (410) 569-0795
Fax: (410) 569-2346
E-Mail: office@ahvma.org
www.ahvma.org

American Veterinary Medical Association (AVMA)
1931 North Meacham Road, Suite 100
Schaumburg, IL 60173-4360
Telephone: (847) 925-8070
Fax: (847) 925-1329
E-Mail: avmainfo@avma.org
www.avma.org

ASPCA Animal Poison Control Center
Telephone: (888) 426-4435
www.aspca.org

British Veterinary Association (BVA)
7 Mansfield Street
London
W1G 9NQ
Telephone: 0207 636 6541
Fax: 0207 908 6349
E-Mail: bvahq@bva.co.uk
www.bva.co.uk

Canine Eye Registration Foundation (CERF)
VMDB/CERF
1717 Philo Rd
P O Box 3007
Urbana, IL 61803-3007
Telephone: (217) 693-4800
Fax: (217) 693-4801
E-Mail: CERF@vmbd.org
www.vmdb.org

Orthopedic Foundation for Animals (OFA)
2300 NE Nifong Blvd
Columbus, Missouri 65201-3856
Telephone: (573) 442-0418
Fax: (573) 875-5073
Email: ofa@offa.org
www.offa.org

US Food and Drug Administration Center for Veterinary Medicine (CVM)
7519 Standish Place
HFV-12
Rockville, MD 20855-0001
Telephone: (240) 276-9300 or (888) INFO-FDA
http://www.fda.gov/cvm

Publications

Books

Anderson, Teoti. *The Super Simple Guide to Housetraining*. Neptune City: TFH Publications, 2004.

Anne, Jonna, with Mary Straus. *The Healthy Dog Cookbook: 50 Nutritious and Delicious Recipes Your Dog Will Love*. UK: Ivy Press Limited, 2008.

Dainty, Suellen. *50 Games to Play With Your Dog*. UK: Ivy Press Limited, 2007.

Morgan, Diane. *Good Dogkeeping*. Neptune City: TFH Publications, 2005.

Magazines

AKC Family Dog
American Kennel Club
260 Madison Avenue
New York, NY 10016
Telephone: (800) 490-5675
E-Mail: familydog@akc.org
www.akc.org/pubs/familydog

AKC Gazette
American Kennel Club
260 Madison Avenue
New York, NY 10016
Telephone: (800) 533-7323
E-Mail: gazette@akc.org
www.akc.org/pubs/gazette

Dog & Kennel
Pet Publishing, Inc.
7-L Dundas Circle
Greensboro, NC 27407
Telephone: (336) 292-4272
Fax: (336) 292-4272
E-Mail: info@petpublishing.com
www.dogandkennel.com

Dogs Monthly
Ascot House
High Street, Ascot,
Berkshire SL5 7JG
United Kingdom
Telephone: 0870 730 8433
Fax: 0870 730 8431
E-Mail: admin@rtc-associates.freeserve.co.uk
www.corsini.co.uk/dogsmonthly

Websites

Nylabone
www.nylabone.com

TFH Publications, Inc.
www.tfh.com

Index

Note: Boldfaced numbers
indicate illustrations.

Photo Credits

Denise Campione (Shutterstock): 66
Seth Casteel: 13, 131
Bob Denelzen (Shutterstock): 106
Gelpi (Shutterstock): 114
James Stuart Griffith (Shutterstock): 49, 130
H.Tuller (Shutterstock): 32
Rafa Irusta (Shutterstock): 56
JackF (Shutterstock): 47
jerrysa (Shutterstock): 121
Amy Myers (shutterstock): 38
Maksim Nikalayenka (Shutterstock): 119

olly (Shuttersock): 46
South12th Photography (Shutterstock): 41
Shutterstock: 70
Designpro Studio (Shutterstock) front cover, spine
Beth Van Trees (Shutterstock): 1, 22
Lisa Turay (Shutterstock): 28, 60, 62, 91, 107, 108
Aaron Whitney (Shutterstock): 110
Karen Wunderman (Shutterstock): 102
Ishbukar Yalifatar (Shutterstock): 104

All other photos courtesy of Isabelle Francais and
    TFH archives

Acknowledgments

I want to thank the following dog lovers for their help in writing this book:

Rebecca Fenlason and her Rat Terriers

Carmeta French, Warren Mountain Rat Terriers

Valerie Luchsinger, Ratitatt Rat Terriers

Pamela Mills, Secretary, Rat Terrier Club of America

And in particular, Kay Blair, Dog Obedience Instructor, Sterling , VA, and

Randy Custer, D.V.M., Georgetown Pike Veterinary Clinic, Great Falls, VA

About the Author

Judith Tabler lives in Virginia with her family, including her five terriers. She has been writing about dogs for more than 20 years and is dedicated to promoting responsible dog ownership. Her love of Rat Terriers dates back to her childhood on Long Island, not far from President Theodore Roosevelt's Sagamore Hill. It was on a visit there that she first learned about Skip, the President's terrier. When she moved to Virginia, she got to know many Rat Terrier-type dogs who frequented the local stables. She is delighted to have had the chance to write about this exceptional breed at a time they are being recognized by the American Kennel Club (AKC).

NATURAL with added VITAMINS
Nutri Dent® MD
Promotes Optimal Dental Health!

Nylabone®

MADE IN THE USA

Our Mission with Nutri Dent® is to promote optimal dental health for dogs through a
trusted, natural, delicious chew that provides cleaning action...GUARANTEED
to make your dog go wild with anticipation and happiness!!!

Nylabone Products • P.O. Box 427, Neptune, NJ 07754-0427 • 1-800-631-2188 • Fax: 732-988-5466
www.nylabone.com • info@nylabone.com • For more information contact your sales representative or contact us at sales@tfh.com   TS446